REWRITE THE STORY THAT TRIED TO BREAK YOU

AND TURN IT INTO STRATEGIES THAT STICK™

HAILEY EVANS, MBA

This book is dedicated to:

The one who refused to let their story end at the breaking.

You did not come here for inspiration—you came for a way forward.

For the quiet battles you endured when no one noticed.

For the strength you forgot you had.

For the ache that still lingers, and the questions that wake you at 3 a.m.

—the ones you shoulder silently, but bravely.

When life gave no answers, you searched for meaning anyway.

When the world moved on, you stayed and chose to heal.

You are not broken. You are being built.

Instead of asking, "Why me?", I invite you to ask, "What's next?"

*This book is my hand reaching back to say—**you were never invisible. You were never alone.***

May every word remind you that:

You are just one story away from breakthrough...

PRAISE FOR REWRITE THE STORY THAT TRIED TO BREAK YOU

"This memoir holds a mirror to every survivor."

As Hailey's former professor, I have seen her commitment to truth and transformation in action. *Rewrite the Story That Tried to Break You* is not just a story of survival. It is a testament to resilience, honesty, and hope.

Hailey's refusal to be defined by pain will encourage readers to rediscover their own strength. This memoir is a beacon for anyone who has ever wondered if they could make it through their darkest moments.

I am proud to support this remarkable work and the power it offers readers on the path to healing.

Dr. Monica B. Fine

Associate Dean of Student Success

Coastal Carolina University

CONTENTS

PART 2

PART II THE R.E.W.R.I.T.E. FRAMEWORK

THE SEVEN STEPS TO HELP YOU REFRAME
WHAT BROKE YOU—SO YOU CAN RISE IN
STRENGTH, LEAD WITH PURPOSE, AND WALK
IN FREEDOM.

PART 3

PART III THE EPIC FRAMEWORK™

WHEN YOUR STORY STOPS BEING ONLY ABOUT
YOU AND STARTS BECOMING THE LANGUAGE
OF HOPE FOR SOMEONE ELSE.

PART 1

PART I THE BREAKING — STORIES THAT SHAPED ME

BEFORE I BUILT FRAMEWORKS, I LIVED THEM. THESE ARE THE MOMENTS THAT TESTED, REFINED, AND REVEALED THE STORY BENEATH THE SURFACE.

ONE

THE TEST THAT STOLE MY CHILDHOOD

Two Pink Lines

The bathroom light flickered above me, buzzing with that harsh fluorescent hum that made every flaw in the mirror stand out, every shadow look deeper, every truth harder to hide. My hands shook so violently I thought I might drop the stick I was holding. Two pink lines glared back at me. Bright, undeniable, merciless.

The air grew thin, like I had been plunged underwater and could not surface. My chest tightened. My stomach dropped like a stone through the floor. My knees weakened, and I grabbed the counter for balance, terrified I might collapse.

I was the honor student. The straight-A's girl. The youth group leader. The track star. The one who checked all the boxes, who lived up to every expectation, who never disappointed. People pointed me out as the example. I was supposed to graduate an entire year early, polished and prepared, a shining promise of discipline and ambition.

And now, here I stood, staring at proof that all of it had shattered.

"Holy shit," I whispered. The word sliced out of me sharp and foreign, like a jagged piece of glass in my throat. I had never even said "damn" before.

Josh stood beside me, his face pale and frozen, lips parted but silent. He looked like he had been carved out of stone, unable to speak, unable to move.

And all I could think was this: after two years of playing Russian roulette, the bullet had finally landed. Two years of unprotected sex, two years of whispered prayers that maybe we had escaped consequence, two years of clinging to the pull-out method like it was anything more than reckless guessing. Deep down, had we ever really believed it would not come to this?

The pregnancy test trembled in my hand, rattling against the bathroom counter. My life plan, the one I had carried with me since childhood, was gone. Finish high school early. Go to college. Build my career. Get married. Then maybe, someday, think about children. All of it lay in ruins at my feet.

College dreams? Gone.

The admiration of my community? Vanished.

My carefully constructed future? A terrifying blank.

Everything I was supposed to be, everything I had worked for, everything that had defined me as "the good girl," dissolved in the span of a flickering light.

But this story did not begin in that bathroom. It had been set in motion three years earlier, when I asked for an upheaval that uprooted everything I thought I knew about life.

The Phone Call I'll Never Forget

I wandered through the next three days half-present, carrying the secret like a stone in my chest. Every step, every breath, felt heavier with the question I was too afraid to say out loud: *What now?*

On the third afternoon, I called a crisis pregnancy center, my fingers hesitant as I dialed the number. A gentle voice answered, steady and kind, and for the first time since those two pink lines appeared, I let my questions spill out.

She told me her story. An abortion years earlier. The details poured out in vivid pieces I could not unhear. The procedure. The silence that followed. The regret that lingered like a shadow she still carried. She spoke of God's forgiveness, but her voice cracked under the weight of sorrow that had never really left.

When the line went quiet, my stomach turned. I pressed the phone harder to my ear as if I could hold myself up with her words, but all I felt was certainty. I couldn't do it. I couldn't choose that path.

That night, I sat on the edge of my bed, the air heavy around me, my heart pounding like a drum. *Could I really do this? Could I raise a baby when I was barely more than a child myself?* Fear screamed at me, but somewhere deeper, a quieter voice answered back: *This isn't the end of your story. It's just the beginning.*

By the time the sun came up, my resolve had settled. I would keep my baby. Whatever it cost, whatever it meant, I would choose life.

I didn't know then what that choice would demand of me. I only knew I would never look back.

If I were going to keep this baby, I had to survive Montana first.

The Exile I Asked For

Three years earlier, by the time I finished middle school, I had already grown tired of the Florida world where I was supposed to be thriving. The hallways felt like battlefields ruled by cliques, shallow kingdoms of girls with designer handbags and sharp tongues. Their laughter was laced with cruelty, their friendships built on secrets and betrayal. Every day felt like navigating a minefield in knock-off sneakers that never quite matched theirs, trying to slip by unnoticed, praying I would not be the next target.

I had influence with my parents, the kind that only children sometimes wield. My voice carried weight, my pleas often heard. And so I planted a seed that grew quickly: what if we moved back to Montana? Back to where both of them had grown up, back to family, back to the wide-open spaces that had always felt like freedom to me.

Every summer, we returned to Montana for visits, and to me, it had always felt like paradise. The Flathead Valley stretched under skies so vast and blue it felt like standing on the edge of heaven. The lake mirrored the snowcapped mountains, holding them still and steady even when the world around me felt unsteady.

I loved everything about those visits. The rodeos where cowboys wrestled broncos and the air smelled of dirt, sweat, and cotton candy. The county fairs where ranchers judged livestock with the reverence of scholars, while children screamed with delight on rickety carnival rides. The summer gathering where I chased a slippery pig across a muddy pen, coming home smeared in manure but grinning like I had won a blue ribbon.

My cousin Melinda lived on a farm, and I adored spending days there. We rode horses bareback across endless pastures until the wind whipped our hair like banners. Once, I teased a massive bull, thinking I was brave, until he lowered his head and charged. I scrambled over the fence, heart hammering in my throat. Another time, Uncle David asked me to help neuter pigs, a job Melinda conveniently disappeared for. Surprisingly, I did not mind. The messy, gritty work made me feel capable in a way classrooms never had.

Montana felt alive. Florida felt like a cage.

And so I lobbied my parents hard, pressing my case with the passion only a determined only child could summon. Most of our family still lived in the Montana valley, including my grandparents, Brad and Hestell, two of the most beloved people in my life. Their home always smelled like bread rising in the oven, always radiated safety. Their weathered hands told stories of steady faith, humble service, and deep love.

Finally, my parents said yes.

That summer, I flew with my dad to Montana. He left me in the care of my Aunt Mary while he returned to Florida to help my mother wind down their lives there. Aunt Mary, my mother's older sister, had never married nor had children. She had spent thirty years as a missionary in Africa, returning to Montana with the resourcefulness of someone who had learned to make do with little and to find joy in simple routines. She had returned to Kalispell to complete her master's degree and carried herself with the kind of steady practicality that made the world feel ordered, even when mine felt upside down.

Aunt Mary kept to her rhythms. Breakfast at the same wooden table each morning, hours tending her garden with a patience that seemed to stretch beyond time, and a soft hum that always escaped when she turned on her favorite movie, *The Sound of Music*. That was ours too — we would watch Maria twirl across the hills, both of us mouthing the words, hers with a faint smile that showed her gentleness beneath all that self-discipline.

In many ways, she was the perfect fit to take me in. She gave me structure when I was slipping, quiet consistency when I felt lost, and the reminder that love did not always shout. Sometimes, it was steady and quiet, like Aunt Mary herself.

At first, I told myself that Montana was temporary. Florida had been my whole universe: the palm trees swaying in humid breezes, beaches stretching toward the horizon, the Methodist church where I knew every hymn by heart and every family by name. But my father's job was unstable, opportunities drying up like puddles under the sun. Montana seemed like the better choice.

Still, homesickness hit within weeks. I cried into the phone, begging to come home. My dad wanted me back, but my mom refused. "This is for the best," she said.

Temporary has a way of stretching into forever when you are fourteen and everything familiar is 2,000 miles behind you.

Want the exact reflection questions and frameworks that helped me turn trauma into transformation?

Scan this QR code to download the full R.E.W.R.I.T.E. Framework™ + EPIC System — the same tools I used to turn rock bottom into rocket fuel... and guide others through theirs.

Inside, you'll get:

☑ **Guided Reflection Questions** for every chapter in Parts I & II

☑ A one-page **R.E.W.R.I.T.E.™ Cheat Sheet** to reclaim your power

☑ The full **EPIC Framework** to turn healing into impact

These aren't just "nice to have" tools —

They're a **map back to yourself... and forward into purpose.**

Scan me!

Scan to Start Your Rewrite

(*Instant download. No spam. Just soul-level strategies that work.*)

➡ Or visit: **epicimpact.com**

TWO

THE BOY WHO CHOSE ME

A Stranger in My Own Skin

Montana in February was brutal for a Florida girl. The cold did not just sting; it invaded, seeping into bones and joints no matter how many layers I piled on. But the weather was only the first assault.

Flathead High School felt like a fortress. Its halls echoed with years of shared history I hadn't lived, a language I couldn't speak. Most of the students had grown up together since kindergarten, their bonds like closed circles I could never quite slip into.

In Florida, the code was clear: designer jeans, crisp polos, sunglasses perched just so on tanned foreheads—status worn like armor. In Montana, the code was different. They wore Birkenstocks with everything—dresses, sweatpants, even in the snow. Thick leather straps, cork soles, toes bare and unapologetic. It wasn't about polish; it was about ease, belonging without effort.

I had neither. Not the designer sheen of Florida nor the sandal-wearing ease of Montana. I walked the halls in silence, an intruder in the wrong uniform. My parents had cycled me through everything: tennis, gymnastics, soccer, swimming, piano, tap, jazz, ballet. I was athletic by nature, but running was different. Running was my safe place, the one arena where ability mattered more than belonging. So I tried out for track, desperate for something familiar. But even there, I felt out of place.

I was small and compact—a sprinter's body in miniature. In middle school, I'd been known for it: medals lined my shelf, my 4x100 relay team shattered the record at our city-wide meet, and my 50-yard dash of 6.2 seconds was the kind of number people brought up whenever they wanted to see me grin. It defined me, and everyone around me knew it.

None of it mattered here. The Montana girls didn't have trainers; they had long legs that ate the track in languid, efficient strides. They moved as if the ground belonged to them. I could still explode off the blocks, still feel the familiar burn in my hamstrings, but their pony-tails bobbed ahead of me with a casual inevitability I couldn't erase. My medals stayed tucked away in a cardboard box; my reputation from Florida was a story no one here had heard. I ran the same races, counted the same steps, and for the first time I watched my own speed dissolve into the space between us.

Still, I kept training. I made varsity, won a few races and even qualified for the Montana State High School Track Competition both my freshman and sophomore years—only to drop out just weeks before each meet because of debilitating shin splints. I had never trained so hard, and to be that close to finally making a name for myself, only to watch it slip away again, was devastating.

What used to make me feel strong now only reminded me of how far behind I really was.

Academics, once my anchor, became a battlefield. My grades slipped, slowly at first, then in a free fall. The girl who had been an honor student in Florida now stared down a D in ninth-grade English.

I remember sitting frozen when Mr. Henderson called my name to deliver a speech on *Romeo and Juliet*. My mouth went dry. I bent my head, silently mouthing one word: 'no.'"

"Miss Volin?" (That was me.) His voice carried across the silent classroom.

I shook my head. I could not speak. I could not move.

The D that appeared later on my report card felt like a brand, proof that I was no longer who I thought I was.

Aunt Mary tried to encourage me, but her words were steel wrapped in concern. "Just focus on your studies," she told me. As if focus were a switch I could flip back on.

But I was drowning. And I did not know how to ask for help.

The Boy Who Saw Me

I first noticed him at youth group. He leaned against the wall with easy confidence, a small crowd orbiting him as if he were the sun. When he laughed, others laughed. When he spoke, people leaned in.

He was handsome, with sharp features and a grin that could disarm. But it was not his looks that caught me. It was the way he carried himself, like he understood secrets the rest of us were still fumbling through. Part of that certainty came from his faith.

Josh's call to ministry had begun long before I met him. At ten years old, in a small Montana church, he scribbled in his journal while an evangelist preached about surrender. Years later, I would see what he wrote that day: *The preacher started talking about me.* That moment marked him. It was as if God had reached into the pew and claimed him with a certainty that never faded.

That faith—steady and unshaken—blended with his confidence in a way I had never seen in a boy before. It made me feel like he already knew who he was, and I wanted to be near that kind of certainty.

When his eyes met mine across the room, something shifted.

He was only two and a half years older, but for a young teenager, those years stretched wide. He had a truck, a job, and a sense of belonging. I had braces, notebooks, and the kind of loneliness that made me desperate to be chosen.

"You're the girl from Florida," he said, finally stepping toward me. His presence filled the space like light fills a shadow.

"Guilty," I answered, surprised my voice sounded steady.

"I'm Josh," he said, extending a hand hardened from construction work. "You look like you could use a friend."

He was right. I desperately needed a friend. But what I found instead was far more intoxicating, and far more dangerous, than friendship.

North Star or Black Hole?

Josh quickly became the center of my world. He picked me up at the bus stop in his truck, already working heavy machinery and earning his own money like a man twice his age. He carried himself with a confidence that made me feel safe and, for the first time in months, seen.

His family seemed perfect. His mother taught Sunday school with a warmth that made children cling to her words. His father built houses that would stand for generations, as solid as the mountains themselves. They were respected in the community, admired by neighbors, and deeply involved in church. On the surface, Josh was the ideal Christian boyfriend for a girl like me, the kind of match that reassured parents and pastors alike.

But perfection has a way of hiding cracks beneath the surface.

Our connection started with small gestures. His hand finding mine during prayer, his arm slipping around my shoulders as the sun dipped low over the lake, our laughter bubbling in the quiet corners of the youth group. Soon, the innocence unraveled.

"We should not be doing this," I whispered one night, though my body betrayed every word.

"I know," Josh whispered back, his breath warm against my ear. "But I love you. And love makes it different, doesn't it?"

At fifteen, I believed him.

Love was the word that made sin feel holy, the word that turned boundaries into invitations. I told myself that our intentions sanctified our actions, that God must understand, that the rules were not broken if we were committed.

I did not see it then, but I was not revolving around a North Star. I was being pulled into a black hole.

Hidden Lake

I was sixteen and Josh was eighteen. We had been dating a little more than a year when he surprised me on a hike to the Hidden Lake overlook in Glacier National Park. The trail climbed from the Logan Pass Visitor Center onto a raised boardwalk that kept us above late snow and a spreading carpet of glacier lilies. The mountain air felt raw and exposed, and that morning a thick fog settled so close the lake below disappeared. The mist thinned the usual crowds to a few blurred shapes.

At the overlook, he took a small box from his pocket. I tried to act surprised. It was not cinematic. He had not even asked my father. When I got home, my mother asked, "Is that the real McCoy?" They were not celebrating. He had already been the center of my world; the hike at Hidden Lake made it official. I gave them little choice.

Prayers with a Scarlet Letter

Sunday mornings were the hardest. I sat in the pew while Pastor Stromberg preached about purity, and the words fell heavy, sharp as stones hurled straight at my chest. The stained-glass windows glowed with holy light, and I swore Jesus' eyes looked straight through me, exposing every secret.

I wondered if everyone else could see it too — the scarlet letter etched into me, burning hot and unforgiving.

But Sunday afternoons brought Josh, and in his arms I felt whole again. Beautiful. Wanted. Necessary. He made me forget the whispers of shame long enough to breathe.

We spun elaborate justifications. We were in love. We would marry young anyway. Surely God could forgive what was already meant to be.

Yet when night came, when I lay alone in my narrow bed at Aunt Mary's house, guilt crept back in like fog rolling through the valley. I prayed desperate prayers, promising God I would stop, swearing this time would be the last.

And then Josh would smile at me across youth group the next evening, and every vow would crumble like sand against the tide.

My Mother's Suspicion

When my parents finally joined me in Montana, my mother picked up on it right away. Her eyes, sharp and unyielding, lingered on me with suspicion.

"You are spending a lot of time with that boy," she said one evening, her voice clipped with warning.

"Josh is a good influence," I answered quickly, hiding behind the truth that was also a lie. Yes, he had restored some of my confidence. Yes, he made Montana feel like home. But he had also awakened desires I had been taught to steward, had led me into a secret life that pulled me further and further from the girl I used to be.

On the surface, my life looked like it was thriving again. My grades climbed. I poured myself into track with renewed determination, shaving seconds off my times. I made real friends for the first time since leaving Florida. From the outside, I looked like a girl who had finally adjusted.

But beneath the surface, Josh and I played a dangerous game. We pulled apart just long enough to make promises, then fell back together with a force that felt unstoppable.

Everyone Else Knew

The warnings came quietly, from all directions, like whispers carried on the wind.

One night after youth group, the youth pastor's car stopped before pulling into my driveway. He turned to me with eyes that carried both concern and pity. "Hailey," he said gently, "I do not think you know everything about Josh. Please be careful."

Josh's best friend was more blunt. "You are going to get hurt, Hailey. He is not who you think he is."

Even my cousin, who was dating that same best friend, urged me to walk away.

But Josh's eyes silenced them all. When he looked at me, I forgot every warning, every rumor, every shadow that clung to his name. I believed in the Josh who picked me up at the bus stop, who made me laugh until my stomach hurt, who talked about our future with certainty that made it feel real.

I chose to ignore the Josh who kept secrets, the Josh with a reputation I did not want to examine, the Josh who would eventually reveal himself as someone I did not truly know at all.

I believed his shadows were few, easy to outshine with love. I had no idea they would multiply, stretching long across the years until they blotted out the light.

But that reckoning was still years away. For now, there was only love. Intoxicating, consuming, dangerous love that made every risk seem worth it.

The Choice That Wasn't Mine

Josh had earned a partial basketball scholarship to Montana State University. It was eight hours away, which to my lovesick, sixteen-year-old heart might as well have been across the world. This was the chance his family had prayed for, the opportunity that represented years of dedication.

But as fall crept closer, his enthusiasm dimmed. His shoulders slumped when the subject came up, his words filled with weariness.

"I do not want to go," he said one night by the lake. The stars reflected off the water like scattered diamonds. "I do not like school. I would rather work. College feels like a prison I do not want to walk into."

His words should have frightened me. Instead, relief and guilt fought inside me. I wanted him to stay, but I knew college was the door to a better future.

"You have to go," I whispered, though my hands gripped his as tightly as a drowning girl clings to a lifeline.

But Josh had already decided. Days before he was meant to leave, he told his parents he would not go. He would stay in Kalispell and work construction instead.

At the time, I believed he had sacrificed his dream for me. I wore that choice like a crown and a chain, proud yet suffocated. Years later, I would learn the truth. He had been cheating through homeschool, stealing answers from his mother's books, and he wanted no part of the discipline college would demand.

But at sixteen, all I knew was this: Josh had chosen me.

THREE

WIFE BEFORE WOMAN

The Gavel Drop

Just as I thought life was steady, my father made his announcement over dinner. His voice carried the weight of a gavel. "We are moving. Davis, California. It is a good job, great schools, better future."

The words hit like blows. My fragile confidence, my friendships, my place in Montana, my relationship with Josh—all of it was about to be torn away. I begged to stay with my grandmother, to cling to the one bit of stability I had built. My parents refused me that choice.

Davis High was another world entirely. Wealth dripped from its hallways. Designer clothes, summer trips to Europe, and college prep programs that cost more than my parents' annual salary. I was invisible in a place where money spoke louder than character.

I made one friend, the daughter of a Nike executive. She drove a sleek Toyota Supra and lived in a house that looked like a castle, all the way down to the fountains in the front yard that sparkled under the California sun. For a while, she seemed genuine. But one day, I said the wrong thing, and she cut me off completely. From that moment on, I was a ghost in the hallways.

All the ground I'd gained—my grades, my honor-student status—collapsed. Once again, I sat in class mute with anxiety. At night, my jaw bore the strain, teeth grinding until pain bloomed and TMJ set in, proof the cycle had caught me again.

"I want to go home," I whispered to the school counselor, tears filling my eyes. "Back to Montana. Back to my grandmother. Back to what makes sense."

Home felt infinitely precious, impossibly far, like stars shining just beyond the reach of my fingertips.

The Return

That fall semester drifted by in a fog. Then, over Christmas break, Josh came for a visit. As he stepped off the plane, seeing him was like breaking the surface after months underwater. He looked taller, older, steadier. When his calloused hands closed around mine, color rushed back into my gray California world.

But Josh had not come only to visit. He had come with a mission.

Over dinner, he leaned forward with a seriousness that surprised me. "Hailey is not happy here," he told my parents. "Her grandmother needs her. She has a plan to graduate early, to get her life back on track. Sometimes a person just needs to be where they belong."

His words wrapped around my parents like a carefully woven net. My grandmother's health was indeed failing, and the logic appealed to their sense of responsibility. I could finish high school early, care for her, and finally find stability again.

Somehow, impossibly, they said yes.

Returning to Montana felt like slipping back into my own skin after months of wearing something that did not fit. The mountains stood like sentinels waiting to welcome me home. Even the biting cold felt kinder than California's endless, false sunshine.

Running Out of Childhood

Once back in Kalispell, I did not waste a second. I was determined to prove that California had not broken me, that I was still the honor student, the girl destined for success.

Seventeen and relentless, I loaded my schedule with seven classes a day, beginning at 7 a.m., plus two summer courses at the junior college. My guidance counselor leaned back in her chair and frowned as we mapped it out. "Are you sure you can handle this kind of pressure?" she asked, her voice careful, almost motherly.

"Yes," I said with all the certainty of someone who had lost everything once and refused to let it happen again.

Every morning, I rose before dawn, footsteps echoing through empty hallways as I made my way to first class. Every night, I studied until my eyes burned, notebooks filled with meticulous notes that proved to me I was not broken, that I still had what it took.

I was racing against time. Childhood was slipping through my fingers, and I was determined to leave something behind that looked like achievement.

But even in the midst of the grind, there was Josh. Always Josh. My comfort, my reward, my undoing.

Our relationship reignited with intensity, fueled by the months of separation and the desperation of young love. The same dangerous intimacy returned. We promised ourselves we would stop, then broke that promise within days. We bought condoms in a panicked rush after one scare, but deep down we both knew we were still playing with fire.

Josh's mom sensed the potential for disaster and insisted we begin Christian premarital counseling to head it off. Josh and I desperately wanted to marry the summer after I graduated high school, but my parents urged us to wait at least another two years. So every other week, we met with the church counselor for sessions on biblical marriage and communication.

For four months, we sat in that office discussing love, faith, and commitment, never once mentioning the giant secret we carried—that we were already sexually active. It felt like standing on a train track, hearing the rumble in the distance, knowing what was coming but refusing to move.

A Moral Map

Before I knew I was pregnant, I carried a clear idea of what a moral life looked like. I grew up in a devout Christian family where abstinence was not just encouraged, it was the answer. Church youth leaders said: *Wait until marriage.* My parents' faith shaped my identity so completely that I believed I would wait too. Still, in middle school and high school, friends talked about sex in ways that made me question everything I had been taught. There was no real conversation at home about how to navigate those choices, only one rule to follow. That absence left me unready for the places life would push me.

When the Test Turned Positive

When the test turned positive in May of 1996, the tidy moral lesson I had carried collided with a messy, very human mistake. I felt I had failed spiritually and morally. My first fear was for my parents and for the church. My mother's worry about appearances tightened my chest.

I did not tell my parents myself. I let our counselor, who had tried to coach us, break the news because I was terrified of how my mother would react. I was right to worry. Her response was worse than I had feared. She even hinted at legal action against Josh. That stunned me. It felt like betrayal from a place that should have been shelter.

I was living with my grandmother at the time. When I told her, she surprised me with kindness instead of shame. She helped pay for part of the wedding and offered steady support without judgment. Years later, when I found her Bible, dates and notations suggested she, too, had been pregnant before marriage. I wished she had told me then. That knowledge would have made the secret less heavy.

In our community, a shotgun wedding was not scandalous so much as practical. Heaven forbid a Christian girl starting showing before she was married. People would whisper the truth. Both sets of parents stepped in to plan the ceremony, not to grant a dream but to stop gossip and protect appearances. The result felt like damage control more than a celebration.

There were only a few dress shops in town, and nothing matched the image I had in my head. Ordering a gown would have taken weeks and cost more than we had, so I chose a white dress with puffy sleeves that fit, but didn't feel like me. I hated it. I had dreamed of something ivory and simple. There would be no fairy tale wedding, the kind that every little girl wishes for.

Because I was underage, county rules required counseling before we could marry. The official steps felt humiliating, another public airing of a private failure. Still, we pushed forward. We married three days before my high school graduation in a small church in Whitefish, Montana. It rained in a thin, steady way that matched the strange mix of grief and hope inside me.

The photographer warned the white satin shoes would discolor in the rain, so for the walk by Whitefish Lake, I swapped them for Birkenstocks. Two years earlier, I had never heard of Birkenstocks. Now I was wearing them. Only immediate family attended. No cousins, no aunts, no uncles. Their absence hurt my parents, and it hurt me.

Watching from the Bleachers

Three days later, I sat in the bleachers while my classmates accepted diplomas. My name was not called; I still had two college classes to finish that summer for dual credit. I had worked to graduate early and wanted that recognition. Instead, I watched from the sidelines, a child bride waiting to graduate. The ceremony felt stolen. The shame of that day lingered long after the wedding flowers had dried.

The honor student. The good girl. The youth leader. The girl who was supposed to walk across that stage and step into college and a future bright with promise.

Now, just another statistic. Another teenage pregnancy. It would take years of wrestling with my shame and regret before I could forgive myself.

Making a Home, Making Do

We rented a small single-wide trailer about ten minutes out of town. Josh worked long hours. He had a fierce work ethic and wanted to provide for his family. He chased contracts and took the jobs that paid the most.

I, newly married and newly pregnant, tried to balance the hope of being a stay-at-home mom with the reality of textbooks, bills, and prenatal appointments. We needed help to cover prenatal care and the birth, but Josh's pay was just high enough for us to be ineligible for public assistance.

Love, Duty, and Doubt

Even then, I lived inside both love and loss. I believed our family could work because we were committed to church, to one another, and to a plan. I wanted to give my children the steady home I had imagined. I wanted to honor the faith that shaped me. Looking back, I see how much fear, pride, and desperation shaped those early choices. I also see small mercies: my grandmother's quiet support, and a husband who, for a time, was determined to do his best.

Those early months set the pattern for what came next. I was young and scared and trying, in clumsy ways, to keep faith with the life opening before me. Josh and I thought the wedding and the baby would be the end of the hard work. Instead, they were the beginning.

The positive test marked the end of my childhood. The birth marked the beginning of survival. For weeks, I lived under a small, private weather system: shame that would not leave, trips to doctors that left my head spinning, nights of whispered prayers that my baby would be alright. By the time the white snow came, I was already braced for something I could not name. A storm was on its way, and I had no idea how hard it would hit.

FOUR

BORN INTO THE STORM

The Lie, the Blizzard, and the Baby Who Saved Me

The lights wrapped around my newborn son made him look like a Christmas ornament. Fragile. Glowing. Tethered by tubes and silence. I sat in the rocking chair beside his wooden cradle in the nursery, praying for a miracle. I could not stop thinking, he came too early, just like everything else in my life.

Just a week before, I was seventeen, thirty-four weeks pregnant, and trying to survive another freezing Montana winter in a single-wide trailer tucked between pastures and snowdrifts. Josh had just gotten home from a forty-eight-hour snowplowing shift. He was passed out cold. I didn't want to wake him.

But something felt off.

I woke up in the middle of the night and noticed a faint pink tint in my urine. I almost ignored it, but something inside me said, *Call.* The nurse at the hospital didn't sound alarmed, but she urged me to come in anyway. The roads were a sheet of ice. I looked over at Josh, sleeping deeply. I almost got in the car myself.

"Josh," I whispered, nudging him. "I think I need to go in."

He blinked. "Are you okay?"

"I don't know. The nurse said to come."

We packed a small bag. Ten minutes later, contractions slammed into me like waves. By the time we reached the hospital, I was already dilated to a six.

Andrew was coming. Fast.

It was still blizzarding outside the car. But the truth was, the storm had started long before that night.

Just days earlier, I had gone to a routine OBGYN appointment. I felt healthy. I felt fine. But my doctor came in with a chart in her hand and a shadow in her eyes. "You tested positive for an STD," she said gently.

I stared at her. Confused. I had only ever been with Josh. He had promised me the same.

I left that appointment with more questions than answers and went straight to the library. I checked out every book I could find about STDs and pregnancy. What I read terrified me.

That night, I confronted Josh. "Is there something you need to tell me?"

He didn't deny it. He confessed to a relationship while I was away in California. We had been engaged. He had lied.

The betrayal cracked something open in me. I felt grief. Rage. Shame. And then, a few days later, my body gave out.

Andrew was born on December 23rd and weighed just 5 pounds, 13 ounces. He had bright red hair and a tiny crooked pinky finger just like his dad's. When I held him, it felt like time stopped. It didn't matter how he got here. He was here. And he was mine.

But motherhood didn't come gently.

Andrew was premature. He had a fever. The nurses whisked him away for tests. I sat in that sterile room, listening to his tiny screams down the hall, aching to do something—anything—to help him.

We had planned to bring him home right away, but the doctor said no. His fever meant another night in the hospital. I nodded, numb. At home, the nursery wasn't even ready. The carpets were being cleaned that day. We had nowhere to go.

On Christmas Day, we were finally discharged. But nursing wasn't working. Andrew couldn't latch. He cried constantly. So did I. I felt like a failure.

The next week, jaundice set in. We tried placing him in the sunlight, but it wasn't enough. We had to rent special lights and wrap them around his fragile body. Seeing him like that, with cords tangled around his tiny frame, broke me in a way I didn't know was possible.

Eventually, I saw a lactation consultant. She gave me a contraption to help him latch. It took a month, but one day, he finally did it. He latched. He fed. And I cried again—but this time, with relief.

I doted on Andrew with everything I had. Every feeding, every fever, every second of sleep lost was a declaration: *I am your mother, and I will never give up on you.*

Josh worked long hours. Money was tight. We had no degree, no plan, and no backup. Just this little boy who changed everything.

Montana was cold. So was our marriage. But Andrew—he was warm. He was my why.

Motherhood didn't ask if I was ready. It came early. Just like Andrew. But it also came with fire. It came with love deeper than anything I had known. It came with strength I didn't know I had.

And yes, my college dreams had been put on hold the moment I saw that positive pregnancy test. I was supposed to be finishing finals, walking at graduation, chasing the career I had planned since I was a little girl. Instead, I was chasing feedings and wiping away tears in a rocking chair.

But even with all I lost, Andrew was never a mistake. He was the best thing that ever happened to me. He was the reason I kept going when everything else in my life felt like it was crumbling.

This chapter of my life didn't start in a hospital. It started with a lie. It started with a blizzard. It started with a baby fighting for his breath.

But it ended with light.

Because Andrew wasn't just born into the storm.

He became the reason I survived it.

A New Kind of Loneliness

But survival in Montana wasn't enough. The storm never really passed—it just shifted.

The job offer came through a man Josh met on the softball field—an equipment company in Washington looking for hard workers. On paper, it sounded like the kind of opportunity we couldn't turn down: better pay, steadier hours, the possibility of getting ahead. Montana was beautiful but brutal. The long winters left Josh plowing snow to make ends meet, and no matter how hard he worked, the dollars never stretched far enough.

I wanted to believe this move would change everything. I told myself: *new place, new start, maybe even a chance to feel normal.* But in truth, I was terrified.

We didn't have much to our name—just Josh's Dodge flatbed, my little Honda, and some worn furniture. The night before the move, I sat on the floor of our trailer surrounded by half-packed boxes,

Andrew asleep in the next room, and felt the weight of it all. Was I really ready to leave behind the only home I'd known as a wife and mother?

When it came time, we sold my Honda. I didn't want to. That car represented independence—my freedom to run errands, visit a friend, escape the suffocating walls when the crying got too much. But the truth was simple: we couldn't afford to keep both vehicles.

I remember arguing in the kitchen, the faint smell of formula still clinging to the counters. "Josh, what am I supposed to do without a car?" I asked, my voice sharper than I meant.

He leaned against the counter, rubbing his temples. "We'll figure it out once we get there. Right now, this is the only way."

His words were final, but my chest burned with resentment. It felt like I was being tethered—traded in right alongside my car.

The drive west was long and heavy. Andrew cried in his car seat, the flatbed rattled with our belongings, and my mind spun with silent questions: *Will we really make it there? Will this job even last? What if Seattle isn't the fresh start I'm praying for?*

When we arrived in Woodinville, the apartment was small and plain, a far cry from the open Montana fields. The air was damp, the sky gray, and for weeks, the rain never seemed to stop. I felt swallowed by it. Josh threw himself into his new job, often working late, while I stayed home with Andrew, trapped in a city I didn't know without even a car to take me beyond the four walls.

The isolation was suffocating. Some nights, I rocked Andrew to sleep and stared out the rain-smeared window, wondering if I had made the biggest mistake of my life. I had traded the loneliness of Montana for a new kind of loneliness—one that echoed louder because it came with the false promise of a fresh start.

And yet, glimmers of hope appeared. Josh and I carved out simple date nights at the mall—cheap pizza, a movie, and holding hands like two kids in love. My cousins, who were in college nearby, sometimes watched Andrew, giving me a breather I desperately needed.

But the struggle was always there, humming beneath it all. Every trip to the grocery store required planning around Josh's schedule. Every bill we opened felt like another reminder of how precarious our lives were.

Moving to Seattle didn't solve our problems. It only reshuffled them. And in the quiet hours, when Andrew finally slept, I wrestled with the same gnawing question: *How long can we really hold this together?*

FIVE

BEFORE HIS TIME

The Baby Who Wouldn't Wait, and the Storm That Wouldn't Settle

I knew it before the nurse said a word. This baby was trying to come early.

By the time I carried Alex, I carried Andrew's birth inside me too, a fast and frightening memory that lived like a warning under my ribs. I was nineteen, still a teenager in many ways, but already carrying the weight of marriage, motherhood, and an income that never seemed to stretch far enough to cover the essentials.

We told ourselves this pregnancy was planned. Andrew was two now —all edges and energy—and I believed a sibling would make our family feel complete. I tried to hold life steady: walking with Andrew to the park, showing up at MOPS (Mothers of Preschoolers, now called MomCo), where I led a small discussion group. I was younger and less practiced than most of the women there, but their kindness offered me a fragile sense of belonging, a rhythm I could lean into.

Then spring arrived. I was outside, pulling weeds along the three-foot rock wall that edged our driveway, when I lost my footing and tumbled backward. Old instincts from gymnastics kicked in. I rolled to absorb the fall and laughed it off, brushed the dirt from my jeans, and thought little of it.

The next day, the contractions began: soft, easy to dismiss. Other moms talked about Braxton Hicks so often that I told myself that was all this was. I had never felt them with Andrew, so I did not know what to expect. Still, a small knot of unease lodged in my chest.

At my next appointment, the doctor frowned. "You are measuring small," she said. "You need more calories and less movement." Her eyes skimmed me the way a teacher scans a student. I almost laughed. Gaining weight with a toddler felt like a fantasy. I worried less about my figure and more about the baby.

By May, the contractions had sharpened into a steady rhythm. I told the doctor how often they came. Her tone changed. "Those are not practice contractions," she said. "Those are real." She checked, and my body gave the truth away: dilated to a three with two months left on the calendar.

Fear settled like a stone. From the beginning, I had said this baby might come early. She had brushed it aside. Now my body proved me right.

Orders followed: Rest. Prescriptions. No movement beyond the basics. After the appointment, I walked into the house pale and shaken. Josh's mother was visiting and caught my face before I could speak. I barely made it to the bedroom and collapsed into the mattress. Within an hour, contractions came in waves I could not deny.

Josh drove me to the hospital. The May sun streamed through the windows while inside me, contractions tightened and quickened. By the time we reached the emergency room, the nurses had moved from calm to quiet urgency. Thirty-two weeks, they said. Too soon.

They gave me magnesium to stop the labor. The drug made my body heavy and strange, like moving through thick water. The monitor beeped at my side, a small, steady metronome that measured time in breath and prayer.

A nurse bent close and lowered her voice. "If the labor can't be stopped, we will transfer you by ambulance to Seattle. But we will do everything we can so that does not happen." I tried to believe her.

Six days blurred into ceiling tiles, IV drips, antiseptic. Josh visited when he could. Someone else kept Andrew. Church families brought casseroles and left them in the hall. Each afternoon, Josh appeared with a small pack of M&Ms and set it by the bed. It was a small thing, almost ridiculous, and yet it reminded me that life existed outside that sterile room.

Eventually, they sent me home with strict limits. Five more weeks of rising only to shower or shuffle to the bathroom. Bed rest became a slow confinement. Friends visited. Hugs happened. The hours moved like molasses, and the waiting cut sharper than pain.

Meanwhile, Josh was anything but still. Now twenty-one, he had decided to start an excavating business. Fear of debt did not seem to bother him in the way it bothered me. He signed loans, bought heavy equipment, and dove into a life of machines. At first, he had a partner who handled the books. Not long after, the partnership unraveled into lawsuits and accusations I could not parse. Fraud. Money missing. The words felt unreal until the bills started arriving.

I lay in bed trying not to trigger contractions while Josh fought a collapsing business from the seat of a bulldozer. I had nowhere to go but inward, conserving strength for the baby inside me. Josh moved outward, trying to keep our life from caving in before it had begun.

May 31 arrived. Our third anniversary. Josh left for a ballgame with a friend. I stayed home with my hand on my swollen belly, trying not to fall apart. In some private corners of my mind, I felt I had earned his slight. After discovering Josh's infidelity during our engagement, I had been foolish and vulnerable. For a time, I let myself wonder what it would be like with someone else. That wondering became two brief flings during our marriage, eight weeks in total. They were wrong. I confessed. They ended. I regretted them and wished I could pull those choices out of time.

His anger, once marked by a fist through the pantry door, was part of the storm we both tried to weather.

In the final weeks of bed rest, desperation makes you reckless. Late in that stretch, I mixed a tablespoon of castor oil into orange juice, hoping to coax contractions to finish what they had started. Josh thought it funny to double the dose without telling me. Within hours, the contractions came back hard and steady, and this time nothing slowed them.

At the hospital, a nurse pushed an IV needle so hard it hit a nerve. My hand burned for nine months afterward. Demerol dulled it a little. "You are at a nine," she said on her next check. There was no time for the doctor. The world narrowed to breath, antiseptic, and the fluorescent hum.

Forty-three minutes later, on June 26, 1999, Alex arrived.

He was not small or frail. In those seven weeks of enforced stillness, he had gained nearly four pounds. Steroid injections had plumped his cheeks and filled out his limbs. We nicknamed him "roid baby," a laugh that came out of relief more than humor.

His nose was bruised from pressing so low for so long. His skin was puffy. He cried. He breathed. Something inside me finally loosened the knot I had been holding for months.

I did not yet know the sleepless nights, the feeding fights, or the weight of postpartum waves that would test me more than anything had before. In that moment, none of it had arrived. He was here. He was safe. That was enough for a while.

Relief does not last forever. It is the eye of the storm, not the end of it. Motherhood began to show me how fierce its weather could be.

SIX

WHAT BROKE ME, WHAT HELD ME

When Enough Isn't Enough

From the first hour, I knew he would test me in ways Andrew never had. Where Andrew slipped into long naps and gentle rhythms, Alex brought a different cadence entirely.

He nursed for only minutes before drifting into shallow sleep against my chest, only to wake minutes later, restless and hungry again. His cries were high and unrelenting, a piercing thread that stitched itself into every corner of the room. By the end of each feeding, I felt scraped thin.

Sleep unraveled. It came in fragments too brief to gather rest, and the erosion showed in my skin and spirit. I moved through the days in a fog heavy with weariness and the sharp edges of shame. Thoughts surfaced that frightened me—brief flashes of silence, of what it might feel like to not be needed so constantly. I didn't have words for it then. Only later would I call it by its name: postpartum depression.

In that season, all I knew was the daily struggle to soothe a baby who would not settle and the quiet ache of wondering why something that seemed to come naturally to others felt impossible for me.

It was Andrew who held me together. Even at two years old, his presence anchored me. He brought me blankets without being asked, patted Alex's back with toddler solemnity, and steadied me with his tiny hand on my arm during afternoons when I felt myself slipping. His small gestures saved me in ways I could not explain.

What Josh Couldn't Unsee

Just when I thought I could not fracture further, the phone rang.

Josh's voice was tight when he told me. He had found his best friend, Dave, in his truck, the engine still running, the garage door closed. The image of it clung to him, a trauma he could not shake. Suicide.

The news swept into our house like a cold wind through an open door. Josh folded inward, grief settling behind his eyes where words could not reach. He wandered through the house quietly, carrying a heaviness I could not lift.

We grieved differently. My body was still bleeding and raw from birth. My mind was chained to Alex's hunger cries and my own cracked nipples. Josh disappeared into what-ifs and unanswerable questions. Between us, silence grew.

The kitchen, once filled with the ordinary noise of family life, became a hollow space where grief pressed into the corners. I spent long hours on the couch, one baby in my arms, another at my feet, wondering how sorrow could divide a marriage not with loud fights, but with the aching distance of two people unable to reach each other.

What the Doctor Took From Me

At eight weeks postpartum, my body gave way.

Alex still didn't nurse well, never feeding long enough to be satisfied. My breasts burned with inflammation, swollen and tender to the lightest touch. Every feeding session ended in tears, sometimes his, sometimes mine.

I tried everything. Nipple shields. Pumps. Ice packs that numbed the pain and warm compresses that promised relief. A lactation consultant adjusted my hold with kind hands, but nothing changed. In the quiet hours of night, I learned to hand-express milk into the sink, the drip loud in the dark, like evidence of failure.

At the doctor's office, her face shifted as she examined me. Her voice turned firm. "You have to stop nursing," she said. "If you don't, we may need to discuss removing tissue."

Her words fell like stones. Nursing had been more than sustenance. It was my last fragile link to feeling like a capable mother. To be told it had to end felt like another failure I had no words for.

I pressed on, stubborn and desperate. I pumped through cracked skin. I swallowed antibiotics and supplements. I watched bottles drain empty while Alex still wailed with hunger.

At three months, I stopped.

Weaning brought grief that settled deep in my chest, but also a flicker of relief that made me ashamed. At MOPS meetings, when the question floated through the air—"Are you still breastfeeding?"—it landed like judgment, no matter how gently asked.

The Role I Never Saw Coming

That fall brought something I never expected. The year before, I had served as a care group leader for our local MOPS chapter, guiding just a handful of women around a table. Others noticed in me what I could not yet recognize in myself: natural leadership and a genuine care for encouraging other women. By the next fall, with Alex four months old, I was promoted to care group coordinator, responsible for organizing other leaders and keeping the circles running smoothly.

By 2001, I had stepped into the role of program coordinator, overseeing a team of twenty volunteers, planning weekly meetings for fifty women, and arranging childcare for nearly seventy children. Most of the women I led were old enough to be my mother, which made the responsibility almost laughable at first. But week after week, I grew into it. Those meetings smelled of coffee and Cheerios, toys clattering in plastic bins while voices rose and softened around tables. For two years, I built schedules, memorized names, and redirected conversations before they soured into division.

Leadership did not erase the chaos at home, but it gave me something else: a place where I was not just the girl who had gotten pregnant too young. I was capable. I was trusted. I was seen. With every meeting I led, confidence grew in me like muscle memory.

It planted a quiet conviction. If I could lead here, I could lead anywhere. If I could carry this, maybe I really could build a career one day. The thought of returning to college still ached inside me, but for the first time, the ache felt less like a wound and more like a waiting dream.

The Boundary That Healed Me

Leadership came with conflict. By the spring of 2000, I was managing a team of eight women, each with a distinct role—hospitality, childcare, curriculum, prayer support, outreach, and finance. They all depended on my direction and expected my leadership to hold everything together.

But leadership rarely moves in straight lines. Heather, who had stepped into my former role as care group coordinator, began stirring unrest. She challenged me in public meetings, whispered gossip in private corners, and cracked open fragile friendships with careless words. I lay awake at night replaying conversations, calling women to sound them out, and wondering if I really had what it took to lead.

Eventually, I made the call. Heather needed to step down. The conversation was hard. Her voice rose, mine trembled, but I held my ground.

The next morning, something astonishing happened. The chronic pain that had gripped my neck and shoulders for months was gone. Just...gone. I had carried babies, hauled car seats, and slept crooked on couches, but this pain had come from somewhere deeper. It was the weight of holding too much, too quietly.

By speaking the truth, my body released what it had clutched for so long.

I could not have known then how much leadership would teach me—not just about programs or planning, but about presence. About how truth, spoken gently but firmly, could heal not only situations but also the body that carried the weight of them.

Storms rarely come one at a time, but neither do the anchors that hold you through them. Sometimes they come as a toddler's hand on your arm. Sometimes as the courage to speak a hard truth. And sometimes in realizing that even broken voices still carry strength.

I thought the hardest storms were behind us. Instead, they were only gathering strength—and the first cracks would appear in the very foundation we had staked our future on: Josh's business.

SEVEN

THE DEBT OF BETRAYAL

Digging Before We Could Stand

By the time Andrew was a toddler and Alex still in diapers, Josh's business had already begun its freefall. The lawsuits from his old partner circled us like vultures, demanding money we did not have. Strangers began showing up at our front door, stiff papers in hand, their voices flat and practiced, "You have been served."

It became a grim routine: the knock at the door, the exchange of the envelope, the shame that followed. Every delivery felt like a public declaration of our private collapse. Each bill that landed in the mailbox carried the weight of Josh's choices, and I felt buried beneath numbers I could not control.

In desperation, we took out a home equity loan, fifty thousand dollars, just to get Josh's partner off our backs. Signing those papers felt like handing over what little stability we had left. I felt the weight of that signature in my gut for weeks after.

We had purchased our home only six months earlier, and now even that felt at risk. What was meant to be our safe place, our foundation, had become another fragile piece of ground we could lose.

I thought I could get a job to help out, but with no family nearby to help, childcare would eat up everything I could earn. Each setback felt like being slapped again and again by the consequences of my sin. Believe me, I knew now that my adolescent behavior had been a grave mistake. But did I need to be punished forever over one irresponsible choice? Was my decision going to bring down my husband and babies, too? Was it all my fault?

After a while, I no longer cared about how it started, the loans or the shiny equipment. All I saw now were the consequences of financial responsibility stacked on top of the consequences of sexual indiscretions: creditors calling, envelopes we could not open without a knot in our stomachs, and a business bleeding out all while Josh drove himself harder and harder trying to resuscitate it.

The Convenience Store Secret

By August 2000, strange signs began to appear. Josh started buying milk at a different store. Then hang-up calls began on our landline. My gut told me the truth before I had the evidence in hand. Eventually, I uncovered it: Josh was having an affair with a convenience store clerk.

Andrew was almost three and a half, Alex only fourteen months. I can still see them in the living room that Sunday after church, Andrew clapping while Alex stumbled into his first steps. Josh wasn't there. He was in a hotel, where I had told him to stay until he could decide what he wanted—a family, or the other woman. I clapped and cheered my toddlers alone while he chased another life.

The Diary That Shattered Me

Then came the third betrayal. In the spring of 2001, I began to notice something unsettling between Josh and a fifteen-year-old girl on our church worship team. Then, her mother discovered a diary filled with descriptions of their relationship, along with unexplained gifts and sightings of Josh's truck at the girl's high school and parked outside her home.

We held a meeting in our house—Josh, the girl, her parents, our pastor, and me. For nearly two hours, she denied everything. Josh denied everything. But I had heard enough detail to feel sick.

Back then, I'd never heard the term *grooming*. Almost no one had. But I knew what he was up to. After all, I'd been through it, too. I excused myself, went downstairs, and sobbed until my body shook.

The worst part wasn't just Josh's betrayal. It was the church's response. They disciplined her—a child—while Josh faced no consequences. She was removed from the worship team, shamed, and wounded. He continued as if nothing had happened. That injustice still makes my stomach turn.

At the time, I told myself this was just another crack in the marriage we might somehow patch. I thought if I just worked harder—prayed harder—maybe I could glue the pieces back together. Why? Because I was still clinging to the hope that our marriage, our family, our life could be redeemed. Because admitting it couldn't also meant admitting my whole world was built on lies.

In truth, I felt trapped. I was twenty-two years old, with a four-year-old and a two-year-old at home. No college degree. No work experience. How could I possibly imagine supporting myself? The weight of that question kept me bound to a life that was already shattering.

I didn't yet realize how many cracks there already were, or how many more would follow.

The Weight of His Highs and Lows

In August 2003, the business finally collapsed. We filed for bankruptcy. It was humiliating. Everyone in town knew us, knew the business, knew it had failed. Worse, small local companies that had trusted Josh were left unpaid. The shame pressed down until I could hardly breathe.

I swore then I would never again be enslaved to debt—mortgage to the hilt, loans stacked like bricks on our backs. Never again!

Only later did we receive an explanation that made some sense of the chaos. Josh was diagnosed with bipolar disorder. Suddenly, the pattern I had lived with for years became clearer. The highs filled with grand ideas, impulsive spending, and sleepless energy. The lows left him withdrawn, irritable, unreachable.

His motto? *Start fast. Borrow big. Crash hard. Repeat.*

He could outwork anyone, but he could not hold steady.

The Hardest No

As the housewife and stay-at-home mom, I tried to be the calm center in the storm, but the chaos made it impossible to breathe. When another business opportunity arose, I took a step I had never taken before.

I picked up the phone myself. I called the man who wanted to partner with Josh and told him the truth. I told him about his history, the instability, and the toll it had taken on our family. I told him Josh was not the right partner. Not now. Not like this.

It was one of the hardest, clearest decisions I had ever made.

I'm proud I did it.

EIGHT

THE CALL THAT WOULD NOT LET GO

Provision, Performance, and the Price of Trust

The boxes came first. They lined our garage in uneven towers, some carefully labeled in black marker, others spilling over with things we could not quite sort. Every time I walked past them, I felt the weight of transition pressing in. We were leaving one failed season behind, though I was not sure yet what we were stepping into.

By the fall of 2003, we were clawing our way out of bankruptcy and betrayal. I had finally made it back into college classes, determined to rebuild something steady after years of chaos. But even in the struggle, Josh found money for something he had been urging me toward for a year: breast implants.

At first, I resisted, ashamed to spend thousands on myself while we were recovering from financial ruin, but he insisted. I told myself that maybe if I said yes, if I changed for him, it might still be possible to keep our marriage intact, that perhaps this would finally calm his wandering eye.

The Trophy Wife Illusion

I did all the things I thought might win Josh's attention. I grew my hair long and colored it blonde, believing that maybe I would look more like the women he admired. After I had Andrew, I cut it short for the sake of convenience. He called me "Butch" for months until it grew out. The nickname stung, and the sting never left.

So naturally, when breast implants were suggested, they seemed like the next step. Long hair, tan skin, blonde highlights, and now breasts to match. The perfect trophy wife. The problem was, the trophy cost me myself.

I smiled for other people. I said yes when I should have said no. I made myself smaller to keep the peace, to keep him happy. I had undergone the surgery because mirrors, compliments, and a husband's praise felt worth the trade. I wanted to feel wanted again. I never imagined the price would be my well-being.

I blamed myself, as always.

Between Collapse and Calling

We rented out our house, packed everything we owned, and in December 2003, moved back to Montana, settling into Josh's parents' basement while we figured out our next steps. Most of our belongings went into storage, since the basement was already furnished. It felt like a retreat and a regression all at once—leaving behind the wreckage of bankruptcy, betrayal, and desperate striving, yet unsure of what would come next.

Both of us were drained from the chaos of the past several years, but in those quiet months, the idea of ministry returned. First in late-night conversations, then in tentative plans, until slowly, a vision emerged: a golf ministry that could weave together Josh's love for the game with outreach and discipleship.

Josh had carried a call to ministry since boyhood, a certainty scribbled in the pages of his childhood journal. For years, it lay beneath the surface, a quiet current even when life veered into shadows. Now, in Montana, that same current began to rise again, tugging us toward a future we had not yet dared to imagine.

Josh picked up part-time work in sales for his parents' building company so we could cover expenses, while I took over grocery shopping, cooking, and meals for the household in exchange for living rent-free. His parents welcomed us, but the house was strained, filled with fault lines none of us wanted to name.

Upstairs, their marriage was quietly unraveling. After thirty years together, Josh's mother would soon pack her things and file for divorce. Living beneath that roof while their relationship disintegrated was suffocating. It confirmed what I had only suspected: Josh had not created his patterns of betrayal out of thin air. He had grown up watching them. The cracks in our marriage felt eerily familiar to the fractures above us.

Downstairs, I tried to give the boys a sense of stability. Andrew started first grade mid-year at the elementary school at the bottom of the hill, the same one Josh had once attended. I drove him through the car line for drop-off and pick-up, just as Josh's parents had done for him years earlier. The routine carried a quiet nostalgia, like watching history repeat itself in a gentler way.

Andrew handled the transition with ease, proving himself responsible and independent far beyond his years. Alex was still home with me full time, and I cherished those slow afternoons with him, filling the quiet with small adventures and ordinary joys.

Our days found rhythm in the basement family room. After laundry cycles finished, I would dump the boys' clean clothes onto the pool table, and together we turned folding into a routine. Andrew quickly learned to pair socks and stack shirts, and even Alex took pride in putting away his things.

I wanted them to grow independent early, to learn how to care for their own space and contribute in small but meaningful ways. Amid the heaviness pressing in from above, those moments of order and responsibility felt like tiny victories.

It was in that uneasy season that Josh began speaking again about ministry. The words carried a kind of familiarity, like something long buried rising back to the surface. I knew the story well by then: the ten-year-old boy in a Montana church, scribbling in his journal while an evangelist preached about surrender. *The preacher started talking about me.* That moment had marked him, and even now, years later, the memory flickered like a pilot light that refused to go out.

Montana became both a refuge and a crucible. The call that had claimed him as a boy was stirring again, and whether we were ready or not, it was already reshaping the course of our lives.

By the fall of 2004, those late-night conversations and tentative plans had turned into a decision. We would take the leap. To prepare, we joined a Family Discipleship Training School with Youth With A Mission (YWAM) in Chico, California. The structure was simple but daunting: three months of training at the base in Chico, followed by two months of overseas outreach.

For us, that meant Fiji—if we could pay for it. YWAM's model is built on personal fundraising. We had no salary or other guarantee, just the hope that friends, family, and strangers would choose to give so that we could serve. Josh, with his silver tongue, could persuade anyone to believe in the dream. Support letters went out, meetings were set, and slowly, envelopes began to arrive.

Montana had been the waiting room, but Chico was the launchpad. The boxes stacked in our garage before we left were proof that we were in transition, caught between what had been and what might be. We were half-rooted, half-restless, asking whether we would dare to trust God for provision.

Josh carried himself differently in those days. His prayers held more focus. His eyes searched for people in need. He noticed what others overlooked and gave quietly, never seeking recognition. He had always been kind and generous, but now, with medication softening the edges of his bipolar disorder, he seemed steadier. After years of business disasters and disappointment, I let myself believe we might be standing at the start of redemption.

What held me back was not the idea of ministry itself but the risk. For eight months, Josh had not held a regular job. We still had two little boys to feed and bills to pay, and I could not imagine how we would stretch what we had. Trusting God to provide felt fragile, like leaning on a bridge I was not sure would hold.

Each envelope built my faith a little stronger, though, until the pile on our kitchen counter was proof enough. God was making a way. For the first time, this did not feel reckless. It felt right. Provided for. Covered. We said yes, not out of blind hope, but because provision confirmed the path was ours to take.

Chico, California greeted us with sun-bleached buildings and air that smelled faintly of dust and hot springs. The former Richard Springs Hotel felt worn but alive, decades of prayers leaving an unseen weight in the walls. Rhythm settled quickly. Mornings filled with worship so loud my chest throbbed. Afternoons packed with lectures. Evenings collapsing into sleep. Andrew and Alex attended the small school on base, laughter echoing down the halls while Josh and I studied discipleship and leadership.

One afternoon, the leaders invited us into a symbolic act of purging. We were asked to bring forward anything from our past that needed to be released, anything that represented sin or bondage, and to throw it into the fire as an offering of surrender. Josh slipped away to our room and returned with a computer disc I had never seen before. He did not explain what was on it, only that it belonged to the old life he was ready to leave behind. As the flames curled around the plastic, I allowed myself to believe he was letting go. Maybe he was not only stepping into ministry, but also walking into freedom.

Later in the training, after we studied the passage where Jesus washed the disciples' feet, the leaders invited us to reflect on humility in action. The room was quiet, filled with the smell of damp carpet and the low hum of fluorescent lights. Without hesitation, Josh stood, grabbed a chair, and motioned for me to sit in front of everyone. Then, with a bowl of water in his hands, he bent down and washed my feet.

The room seemed to hold its breath. People murmured about the beauty of the moment, the picture of Christlike service. And in that instant, it was powerful. I wanted to believe it was as pure as it looked.

At the time, I did not question it. I did not ask about the fire, either, or the disc Josh had thrown into the flames. I wanted to see progress so badly that I chose to believe what he showed me. It was only years later, after the marriage was over, that I looked back and recognized the pattern. His performances of humility, his staged moments of surrender, were often less about transformation and more about convincing me or others that change had come.

But in that season, I pushed those doubts aside and tried to focus on what I thought was growth. And as I did, another storm was quietly beginning. Not in Josh, but in me.

It began as a tightness in my calves, the kind of ache you blame on a treadmill or a long day of standing. I stretched, I iced, I told myself it was nothing. But then the spasms came, sharp jolts that woke me at night, my muscles twisting without release. Soon the ache spread, a slow burn that medicine did not touch. I prayed for relief, but the words felt thin, bouncing off the ceiling like a whisper.

I pressed forward anyway. I learned to share my testimony before large crowds, offer encouragement to those in need, and speak words

I wasn't always sure I believed. I found solace in the smell of coffee and chalk dust, in the steady rhythm of teaching and prayer. Leadership gave me structure when my body was unraveling.

When our three months of training ended, we packed for Fiji. I folded clothes into bags with hope tucked between them, convinced that sunshine and ocean air would loosen whatever had gripped me. I believed heat and salt would heal me, that a change of place might be enough.

At the time, I told myself it was just another season. Only later would I realize it was the beginning of something much larger.

NINE

THE ESCAPE PLAN

When the Island Couldn't Heal Me

The air in Fiji wrapped itself around me like a wet blanket, sticky and relentless. I remember stepping off the bus at the mission base, sweat already running down my back, and watching our boys bolt ahead, their laughter cutting through the heavy air. To them, this was an adventure. Turquoise waters, coconut palms, barefoot soccer games with kids who needed nothing more than a ball and an open field.

Our team of sixteen had traveled from California together, but the leadership had shifted unexpectedly at the last minute. The married couple who were meant to guide us received difficult news just before leaving—one of them had been diagnosed with kidney disease and could no longer take on the responsibility. Instead, Josh was asked to step into the leadership role alongside a woman on our team. He was a natural choice, already respected and steady in the eyes of many. For him, it was confirmation of a calling he carried with confidence. For me, it was one more reason to hope this season might be a turning point.

For Andrew and Alex, Fiji was the kind of childhood magic that leaves an imprint forever. They thrived in that environment, learning to see abundance not in possessions but in people. They prayed for strangers after hearing stories of loss, and at the orphanage they visited, children with almost nothing clung to them with fierce hugs and contagious laughter.

They sat "criss-cross applesauce" with village children, trading pieces of bread and bursts of laughter, and they shared meals with families who lived in one-room homes yet offered us the best they had.

They ran barefoot through villages, hands linked with kids who didn't speak their language but spoke joy fluently. In those moments, they discovered a compassion that widened their world— and even now, they remember it as one of the most special times of their lives.

For me, it was survival.

Our discipleship training had shifted from classrooms in California to this island, where days began with worship and ended with service in villages. I sat cross-legged on woven mats, eating simple meals of cassava and curry while chickens darted around the door. The joy of the Fijian people radiated like sunlight, and their generosity often left me undone.

Life on the island revealed layers of complexity I had never seen before. The native Fijians carried the soul of the land, their culture warm and communal, steeped in tradition and storytelling. Yet much of the land was leased by Indo-Fijians, descendants of Indian laborers brought during British colonial rule. They owned many of the businesses, the small shops that sold spices and fabric, the taxis that wove us through crowded streets. Both communities had their tensions, but what struck me was how, as outsiders, we were welcomed into both worlds. Our taxi driver invited us to his home for tea. A family we met at church insisted that we come and share dinner. Strangers treated us as though we belonged, their hospitality as natural as breathing.

But beneath the surface of those holy moments, I was unraveling.

The pain in my legs had grown from a nagging irritation into something darker. At night, spasms shot through my muscles like electric currents. My calves seized without warning, toes curling, ankles tightening until I could barely move. I was grateful that we had a massage therapist as part of our team, yet even her handiwork gave me no relief. I stretched, prayed, and cried, but nothing helped. I started a course of anti-inflammatories, but they contributed more side effects than solutions. On long walks into villages, my body betrayed me. I often had to stop, sit on a rock, and elevate my feet while others pressed on ahead. I could feel the eyes of people on me, wondering if I was weak, if I was not cut out for this work.

I thanked God that I did not have to walk barefoot to the market each day, like so many Fijian women who carried heavy baskets home just to prepare a single fresh meal, their strength both humbling and convicting as I struggled to take even a few steps.

I hated that thought. So I pushed through, plastered a smile on my face, and told myself this was simply the cost of ministry. Jesus carried a cross. I could carry leg pain. Or so I tried to believe.

The whispers of fear grew louder in the quiet hours after worship, when the boys had fallen asleep on thin mattresses and the humid air hung heavy in the room. My body throbbed with pain while my mind searched for answers. I told myself it was bad shoes or stress. Anything but the truth I did not want to face. Something was deeply wrong.

Then came the tsunami.

It was not in Fiji but across the waters in Malaysia, Thailand, and beyond. December 2004. We watched the news in silence, images of waves swallowing entire coastlines, whole families gone in an instant. Grief rippled across the globe, and even here we felt its weight.

Andrew and Alex sat with us during worship, eyes wide and earnest as they prayed for children they had never met. I saw something change in them during those nights. Compassion took root. Awareness deepened. Their prayers were no longer about toys or simple requests; they carried the burden of a broken world on their young shoulders. That alone made the experience priceless.

I should have been swept up in that same expansion of spirit, but instead I felt myself shrinking. My body tightened, pain pulled me inward, and even as my boys stretched their hearts toward the world, mine curled into itself, desperate for relief from something invisible.

When we finally returned to the States, landing in Sacramento with suitcases stuffed with seashells, sulus, and souvenirs, we had missed both Thanksgiving and Christmas. My parents tried to recreate the holidays for us—a turkey on the table, mashed potatoes, the smell of cinnamon and cloves filling the house. Yet the abundance felt foreign.

I could not stop replaying the words of a Fijian pastor who had joined us for a simple meal: *I have never seen this much food in one place before.* An eight-foot table covered in dishes we would only half eat suddenly seemed obscene. What once felt warm and familiar now struck me as excessive, almost grotesque, when filtered through the lens of what we had just lived.

Fiji had marked us all. For Andrew and Alex, it was a season of child-like joy, widening vision, and unforgettable lessons. For Josh, it was confirmation of his calling, provision unfolding where fear once reigned. For me, it was both—a glimpse of beauty I will always treasure and the beginning of a shadow I could not yet name.

As we packed once more, preparing for what we hoped would be our final move, we began looking south. We wanted a place where golf could be played year-round, where ministry doors might open, and where we could finally put down roots.

South Carolina wasn't on our radar at first, but soon it began to feel like the answer. I carried more than suitcases on that journey—the memory of a once-in-a-lifetime adventure, Josh's vision for what might come next, the boys' wide-eyed wonder, and the growing weight of something my body refused to release.

TEN

WHERE IT FINALLY FELT LIKE HOME

Unpacking More Than Boxes

The summer of 2005, just before Hurricane Katrina struck the Gulf Coast, we packed up our lives once again and headed east. South Carolina was calling.

Josh had officially launched the golf ministry as a full-fledged nonprofit, complete with 501(c)(3) status and a board of directors. It was yet another new venture—this time with my full blessing. The idea had begun as a pilot during our time in Fiji, where Josh used golf trick shots to capture attention before sharing the gospel. The response there convinced him it could be more than a novelty. People listened. Some laughed at the unexpected mix of golf and faith, but most leaned in, curious.

Doors opened for conversations, for testimonies, even for prayer. Still, whenever we explained it back home, the idea often raised eyebrows. "A golf ministry? What does that even mean?" they would ask. Josh would smile and explain that the same skills that amazed a crowd could also serve as a bridge to the deeper message of faith. He believed in it with all his heart.

We wanted to settle in a southern state where golf was played year-round, and when a door opened in South Carolina, the decision made sense. We knew just one family in Anderson, but after visiting, everything seemed to fall into place. Housing was affordable, schools were good, and the culture of the Bible Belt seemed like fertile ground for ministry. For me, the atmosphere carried a familiar rhythm, reminding me of South Florida, where I had grown up.

When we unpacked, it felt like Christmas morning. For eighteen months, we had been living out of suitcases, our belongings packed away in storage while we traveled domestically and internationally. Opening each box, unwrapping dishes, pulling out toys, and placing books back on shelves felt like unearthing little pieces of ourselves that had been tucked away for too long.

The boys adjusted quickly. Andrew started third grade, and Alex began first grade. Both of them made friends easily at school and at church. Andrew had already fallen in love with soccer when he was four years old, and Alex was close behind, determined to keep pace with his big brother. Saturdays filled with soccer games, shin guards, and juice boxes, while weeknights included basketball practices, homework, and church activities. They thrived in every setting—school, sports, friendships, and faith—and watching them was pure joy. They were the best of friends.

Josh's ministry was growing, too. He traveled frequently, performing his show in Hong Kong, Malaysia, Ukraine, Canada and even parts of China. These events often blended ministry with income, allowing him to perform for a corporate crowd and then partner with a local church before returning home. Sometimes I traveled with him, joining him in Hong Kong, Japan, and Ireland. It was refreshing to stand at the back of the crowd, watching him astonish the audience with his trick shots before turning to deliver a clear and meaningful gospel message. It felt as though we were finally in our element, especially him. I found myself thankful that we had endured and somehow made it through the disasters that had plagued us for so many years in Washington.

Together, it seemed like we had stepped into a new season. South Carolina gave us a sense of ordinary rhythm—a neighborhood, a church community, children who were thriving, and a ministry that felt full of possibility. For the first time in a long time, it felt like we were exactly where we were meant to be. One church member later told us, "You opened your home to lead small groups, welcomed college students and young families, and we watched people grow and deepen their relationship with Christ. Your family's presence here made a difference."

But my health continued to spiral. The pain in my legs had not gone away. It had worsened. Sleep became difficult. New symptoms emerged: thyroid imbalances, restless leg syndrome, and a growing sense of fatigue that never lifted. I bounced between doctors and specialists. A rheumatologist ran labs, some abnormal and some normal, but no diagnosis stuck. Not fibromyalgia. Not lupus. Not arthritis. Still, the pain and brain fog were real. They prescribed anti-inflammatories and sent me on my way.

Josh was gone often, and I held the fort, managing the boys, the house, and my increasingly fragile body. Then one day, while Josh was away, I saw something I could not ignore. A canceled plane ticket in the mail, addressed to another woman. My stomach dropped. I started digging deeper. I opened his email and found messages to multiple women.

When I confronted him, he insisted there had been no sexual relationship, only communication. But the plane ticket told a different story. And every time I pressed for more truth, more of the story surfaced. What I learned was this: Josh was excellent at giving just enough information to quiet my questions, but never enough to rebuild trust.

This was the fifth affair that I knew of. Whether it was emotional or physical did not matter to me. Betrayal was betrayal, and I had had enough. I looked him in the eyes and said, "Josh, we are in ministry. We are leaders in our church, pillars in our community. If there is one more affair, I am leaving with the boys."

I meant it. ...Maybe?

ELEVEN

THE BODY THEY DID NOT BELIEVE

The Whisper at the Door

I was on my way out the door to community college, having enrolled in courses again after years of putting myself last. One hand rested on the doorjamb, the other gripped the strap of a school backpack. And then it hit me with such clarity. The thought was small, ridiculous, and undeniable—breast implants.

That morning, Josh was gone again, traveling for work. It had become the norm. Every time there was a crisis, he was absent. Medical emergencies, automotive trouble, health scares, dying pets, bills piling up—I faced them alone. Andrew, only ten, had begun calling himself the man of the house. He was still too young to shoulder that kind of weight, but he did. He buried our 4-H chickens when disease swept through the coop. He dug a grave for the family bunnies when they died. I watched him press small bodies into the earth and thought, "This should not be his job. Where is Josh?"

The Silence of Doctors

The recognition at the front door felt humiliating and stupid. How had I missed what was literally under my nose? As I learned, grief blinds you, and survival teaches you to overlook the obvious.

For years, I had seen the same rheumatologist. Appointment after appointment, he studied my bloodwork, shook his head, and prescribed pills that never solved anything. I never told him about my implants. I was embarrassed, and honestly, it never crossed my mind that there could be a connection.

The surgeon who put them in had assured me they were safe. Saline implants do not cause cancer, he said with such certainty that I accepted it as fact. If one ruptured, he told me, it would be only a little salt water the body would absorb. I could not have imagined that the shell itself might leach toxins, that what looked like harmless saline could hide a very different kind of harm. I never thought to ask about anything else, autoimmune disease or chronic inflammation or the kind of bone-deep fatigue that eats a person alive. Oh God, how could I be so naive?

Two days after the possible connection hit me on the way to class, I sat on the exam table at the rheumatologist's office, staring at the sterile paper crinkling under me, and said, "I think I know what's wrong. I think it's the implants."

The doctor leaned back in his chair, steepled his fingers, and sighed. "I'm not surprised," he said evenly. "I wrote a research paper in medical school about the link between implants and autoimmune disorders."

I stared at him, heat flooding my face. Years of suffering. Years of him watching my body fall apart. "Why didn't you ever bring it up?" I wanted to shout, but the words caught in my throat. Instead, I nodded, too exhausted to fight.

I had carried that silence into his office for years. Hearing him confirm it felt like a delayed strike—relief and anger braided together.

If I had just been open from the start, maybe he would have pieced it together sooner. Maybe he could have spared me some of the years I lost. Instead, I carried the shame of silence, believing my implants had nothing to do with what was happening to my body. I needed to get rid of the artificial part of me if I were ever again going to feel like a human being.

The Surgeon Who Believed Me

The first cosmetic surgeon I saw laughed at me. She leaned in with a kind of condescending curiosity and said, "You are healthy. You will be fine." I walked out of her office feeling smaller than I had in years. Her dismissal hardened me.

My surgeon in Atlanta was different. A bit fruity, some said. Her personal life seemed to be fodder for gossip in certain circles. But I did not care. All I cared about was that she believed me, that she did not look at me like I was inventing my pain. She spoke about my health struggles with respect, not dismissal, and treated explantation as a medical necessity, not cosmetic regret. She agreed to remove the implants intact, to send the capsules for independent analysis, and to treat the removal as the extraction of something that might be harmful.

Vindication and Wounds

The surgery that put them in had been a 45-minute, $3,000 promise to look a little better in a mirror. The surgery that took them out was six hours, $12,000, and a different kind of pain. Recovery took months. For three weeks after, it felt like my chest had been ripped out and trampled. I had drains on each side.

One afternoon, Andrew walked into my room before I could hide them. His eyes went wide. "Mom, are you dying?" he asked.

I froze. To him, the tubes looked like cancer. Like I was leaving him. I wanted to reassure him and laugh it off, but instead, I cried. What have I done to myself? What have I done to my children?

When the lab report came back, it felt like vindication and a new wound. Dr. Pierre Blais' analysis was direct: defective valves on both implants allowed the saline and my body fluid to mix by osmosis, resulting in significantly contaminated fluid in the capsules, with the contamination being much worse on the right side. Reverse osmosis had quietly turned the implants into a cesspool of micro toxins that bathed my tissue for years.

This was not just one doctor's opinion. It was the conclusion of Dr. Pierre Blais, a world-renowned expert in implant safety, whose decades of research have shaped regulatory reviews and led to Congressional testimony. When he said something was wrong, it echoed in the rooms where laws and standards were written.

I printed the report and sat at my kitchen table, reading it until the words blurred. Then, with a quiet kind of fury, I wrote the only letter that made sense to write, an exhausted ledger of what I had lost.

08/07/2008

Dear Dr. Blais,

Thank you for your initial analysis. You noted that the valves were defective on both sides and that the filling fluid was signifi-cantly contaminated, mostly on the right side. This is in line with my symptoms, as they were much more severe on the right side of my body. ... I have spent over $40K on trying to find solu-tions to my health problems, including the very costly explant surgery.

— Hailey

The Fog of Suicide

Yet answers did not cure me. Removal was a beginning, not the end. My body continued to rebel in ways medicine could not always explain, and the silence around my pain was worse than the pain itself.

The pills sat on my nightstand, amber bottles lined up like little soldiers. Antidepressants. Muscle relaxers. Painkillers. None of them had delivered what they promised. None had taken the pain away. But together, I thought, they could silence everything.

I started to picture it. First, the bottles lined up in a row. Then, a glass of water. Then, the quiet after. The steps felt practical, almost tidy.

Lying in bed, I would hear my boys laughing in the next room, their voices bright and full of a life that felt farther and farther from me. A part of me thought, they deserve better. A mom who can drive them to practice and cook them dinner, not this shadow in a bedroom.

The thought did not crash into me like a storm. It came slow and thick, like fog seeping under the door. The kind of fog that makes you forget the shape of things, makes you doubt there is light beyond it.

But even in the fog, something thin held me. A thread of love. A stubborn whisper: *not yet*. I began to imagine days so ordinary they felt dangerous to hope for. Pancake mornings. School recitals. Andrew's high school graduation. Meeting Alex's wife someday. Holding grandchildren who would curl their tiny hands around my finger. Those imagined moments did not erase the pain, but they glowed just enough to keep me tethered.

I did not want to die. I just wanted the unbearable to stop.

The Florida Pilgrimage

The anger came quickly once the fog receded. I had gotten those implants not for me, but to please Josh. They had not fixed anything. They had stolen time and health.

So I chased control. When a doctor emphasized the benefits of juicing and cleansing, I listened. Juice fasting became a discipline. Discipline became obsession. Eventually, I went three full weeks without eating. Water only.

The Florida pilgrimage came after the implants were out. It was the summer of 2009. I had made friends with another wife and mother who had the same constellation of symptoms. We agreed to attend a cleansing program in Florida.

The institute promised to purge whatever demon had possessed our bodies. Three weeks of intensive detoxification. Wheatgrass by the glass. Wheatgrass by enema. At orientation, a staff member beamed and told us, "Your livers will thank you." My friend leaned over and whispered, "Or hate us forever." We laughed, but it was the kind of laugh that cracks at the edges.

The smell of cut grass clung to my hands. The juice was sharp and metallic on my tongue. Each morning, we lined up in a white tiled room that smelled faintly of bleach, holding tiny cups of green liquid. "Bottoms up," one woman said, forcing a grin. By the second week, the jokes ran out.

The enemas were worse. Cold liquid, rubber tubes, fluorescent lights buzzing overhead. Humiliation dressed up as healing. I remember one afternoon, trembling and dizzy, asking my friend, "Do you feel any better?" She shook her head. "Just emptier."

For those unforgettable weeks, I could declare with absolute certainty that I was not full of shit. Not at all. From my head to my butt, I was full of freshly squeezed wheatgrass.

The experience was invasive, humiliating, and useless. Three weeks later, my symptoms remained unchanged. I was thousands of dollars poorer and no closer to understanding what was destroying me.

When Healing Became Harm

The fast turned on me. Severe dehydration and relentless fasting produced a gallstone that went unrecognized for months, leading to gallbladder removal. Another operation, another bill, another scar—all collateral damage from my original choice to get implants.

Pain became a constant companion. I dropped to one hundred pounds.

Nine months after the fast, a gastroenterologist finally ordered an X-ray. It revealed a partial blockage that had not been considered. My body had been so starved and dehydrated that stool had compacted and lodged deep in my intestine.

The fix was humiliating and simple. A bottle of magnesium and a miserable afternoon in radiology with a bucket nearby. It worked. I could eat again.

That moment was a small miracle and a mirror. I saw how intensely I had believed punishment was progress. I saw how I had punished the same body that had been trying to save me all along.

Becoming My Own Archivist

After the humiliation of the cleanses, the real, invisible labor set in. Phone calls with insurers that ended in an automated rejection. Appeals that emptied whatever energy I had left. Lab panels that contradicted each other and raised more questions than answers. Clinicians who either leaned in to listen or glanced at my stack of files and moved on.

I became my own archivist. I labeled receipts, operation notes, implant analysis, lab reports, and emails to physicians. Paper was my armor against doubt. I trusted only the handful of doctors who admitted they did not have all the answers and who promised to keep looking with me.

Slowly, the medical world began to open a door. Case reports multiplied into panels. Panels gave rise to institutional reviews and summaries. The phrase *breast implant illness* started to appear on reputable sites and in academic discussions. Centers once silent were now publishing overviews. Still, recognition did not equal remedy. Implant manufacturers enjoyed legal protections that insulated many from liability, and for countless women, there was no straightforward path to compensation or accountability. Hundreds of thousands had their health, livelihoods, and families altered, often without recourse.

I kept my footing. I stayed in school. I showed up for my boys. I studied anatomy, pharmacology, and whatever else I could to make sense of what had happened to me and to help others avoid the same blind faith.

One Hard-Won Truth

The answers were not tidy. Neither was the science. For me, the convergence of implant analysis, abnormal inflammatory markers, and genotype information formed the most coherent narrative I had in years.

This is not a lament. It is a reckoning. At its center is one hard-won truth: Love your body for itself.

I am not willing to let disbelief be the final word on my pain. I keep the reports. I keep the letters. I keep the scars.

I tell this story not for pity but to give permission. To the woman hesitating before surgery, to the mother shrinking herself to make someone else comfortable, to the person told they are fine when they know they are not, listen to your body. Protect it. Love it for itself.

Back at the front door, where this all began, I set the backpack down. Rain had left a soft fog on the lawn. The fog no longer scares me the way it used to. It used to cover the edges of my life and make them blur. Now it is just weather.

I open the door and the light comes in, thin and honest. I step forward.

TWELVE
HER NAME WAS NADINE

The Chest That Would Not Ease

During the worst of my health struggles, a different pain grew under my ribs. It was not a symptom a doctor could name. It tightened when Josh looked at me and did not tell the whole truth. It sat there while I sipped bone broth and tried to learn the shape of a life with less energy, less certainty, less comfort.

The ache was moral as much as physical. I kept asking myself whether to wake a sleeping thing. If I confronted him, would it blow open a clean wound or set off something worse? Would it push him away, finally, the way absence already had, and leave the boys with two empty sides of a house? Or would silence be a slow poison, a daily eroding that taught the boys that truth could be optional?

I imagined both paths a dozen times. In one version, I asked him to look me in the eye and say only one sentence, "No. I would never do that to you again." That look of certainty could mend something. In another version, asking would start a fight that would not end in apology but in packing, in his suitcase already half zipped because he had practiced leaving. I pictured Andrew staying with a neighbor because his father had left town, and I pictured him burying chickens and bunnies, pretending not to notice the way the house shifted without a steady hand.

I toggled between fear and hope. Protect the boys by not stirring the hornet's nest. Protect the boys by forcing the truth into the light. Every argument had costs. Every argument felt like another illness in the room.

Bone Broth and Broken Promises

Not knowing was another kind of wound. Not knowing let suspicion grow like mold in the corners. Not knowing meant my nights were a loop of questions. Not knowing turned minor oddities into proof in my head. I sat at the kitchen table, the mug of broth growing cold, and began to type because the asking itself felt like a necessary act, a way to stop swallowing suspicion with my food.

Evidence: An Email, May 11, 2010

Josh,

How are you? I did not sleep. My mind will not stop. I keep turning over everything we said and everything we did not.

I am still trying to understand what is going on between you and Nadine. When we met her at the conference, I told you I was not comfortable. At home, the messages between you two did not stop. You said it was about fitness and time management. You said it was nothing. But it felt off.

Then you flew to Canada. You said she was busy running the event, but she picked you up at the airport herself. If I were that busy, I would send a friend. Would most people not do the same?

When I asked you about it, you said she was weathered. That she and her husband were working on things. I needed you to look me in the eyes and say, "No. I would never do that to you again." You did not.

Why did she buy your ticket? Why did she cover your expenses? Why did you take a swimsuit when you almost never do? Why were you on international calls about fundraising when you said those calls were too expensive?

These things do not add up. *You've been distant for months. You said you're having a midlife crisis, and I've tried to give you space to figure it out. But what I see is detachment. Vagueness. Excuses. And when I put those pieces together, they look like something I never wanted to see again.*

If this is your idea of rebuilding trust, it is not working. It feels like I am standing outside a house I used to live in, looking through the windows. I want to believe you. I want to be wrong. But too much does not add up.

Please be honest with me. Have you gotten too close to her? What happened on that trip? Was it about work, or was that only a cover? All I have ever asked is for honesty. I deserve at least that.

Love,

H

The Send and the Silence

Writing the email felt like stepping onto a narrow bridge. Deleting it and saving it as a draft felt like stepping back. I rewrote the opening line five times. I told myself not to accuse. I told myself the boys came first. I told myself that if his answer included leaving, I did not want to hand them that memory of their mother starting a fight she could not finish.

When I finally hit send, it was not triumph. It was an exhausted surrender. The cursor blinked for a long time, each blink a small drumbeat of waiting. I could hear the boys in the next room, the ordinary, small sounds of life that had kept going while mine felt suspended. I imagined the worst. I imagined him denying everything and me losing the little dignity I still held. I imagined him confessing and packing. I imagined the boys waking up and finding one parent gone.

I also imagined the relief of a truth told, ugly as it might be, because truth could at least be met, could at least be acted on. Not knowing had become its own theft. Not knowing had hollowed out days. If the boys were to grow up in a house with honesty at the center, I had to try.

After I sent that email, I walked the kitchen until my legs felt like they'd been walked out from under me. I did not want to eavesdrop on my own life, waiting for his reply. I told myself, over and over, that I had done the only thing left to do. I told myself I had chosen the harder protection for my sons: not the protection of silence, but the protection of seeking truth.

I did not know if that protection would succeed. I only knew I could no longer carry the question in silence.

THIRTEEN
THE QUESTION IN INDIANA

The Woman in the Van

Two months after I had written that email to Josh about Nadine, the question landed in my head like a stone, and everything stopped moving. We were visiting friends in Indiana—Melanie and her husband, who served on the board of Josh's golf ministry—when the words slipped into the room as if they had been waiting there all along.

"Was that the woman sitting next to you in the van?"

Melanie had seen them herself. During the *Bike Across America* trip, when the riders came through her town, she noticed Nadine sitting beside Josh. That memory had lingered, waiting for a place to be spoken. Now, in her own kitchen, she finally gave it voice.

The air thinned. The clink of bottles and children's laughter faded. Josh said *"yes,"* and with that one syllable, the axis of my life shifted.

My hands went cold against the counter. I remember the crock of coffee tipping, liquid spilling across the surface as if time itself had stumbled. The significance of one question and one answer was undeniable: this was the moment I knew our life as we had built it was over.

The Van and the Promise

Before the trip, Josh had told me he was going to join a cross-country bike race as a support person. It started in California and ended on the East Coast. He would drive a van, help the riders, do the work that made the team function. It sounded noble. It also sounded like a good excuse to be away. He had a way of wrapping every absence in mission and calling it service.

I had asked him to keep his distance from Nadine. We had agreed he would not be in the same vehicle as her. Did I trust him? No. Did I hope he would show some integrity after everything that had happened? Maybe. But some part of me still wanted him to be the person he said he wanted to be.

When our friend asked the question that night, my hope shattered. He answered yes quietly, without flourish, and that small, calm assent made the betrayal feel official. He had not balked. He had not explained. He had not contradicted the proof cooked into the words.

The Ultimatum and the Couch

Earlier that spring, I had given him an ultimatum. I had tried to keep our family intact, but I had one line left: *make the change or leave.* That night in Indiana, sitting in someone else's home with the weight of Melanie's question still hanging in the air, I decided I would make good on it.

When we went downstairs to the guest room, he tried to slip into bed beside me, as if nothing momentous had just happened. As his body shifted toward mine, I felt the old muscle memory of being a wife— the reflex to respond and soften. For a second I almost let it come forward. Then I turned, my voice cutting through the quiet.

"What the hell do you think you are doing?"

The words shocked the room into silence. I held his gaze and said, steady and low, "You are on the couch. Go."

I wanted the words to be small enough that our hosts and the kids would not hear, but unmistakable enough that he could not pretend to miss their meaning. He left the room without protest and slept on the couch, like a stranger in someone else's house.

The Drive Home

The next morning, we piled into the car for the long drive back to South Carolina. The boys, now eleven and thirteen, had their earphones in and their world of music between them and the truth. I watched their faces in the rearview mirror, trying to find some sign that they understood. They looked like boys, lost in their playlists, but I felt the tension tighten the air like static.

At a gas station, we pretended to be ordinary. We went inside, ordered fast food, sat at a corner table, and chewed mechanically while our family imploded under the same fluorescent lights. Later, after a ten-hour drive and too many miles of polite silence, the truth that had been contained in texts and receipts spilled out from him in a muted collapse.

He admitted it. He had had an affair again, this time with someone I had once considered a friend. The admission was not cinematic. There was no apology that reached the place where I was hurt. There was only a bleak catalogue and a bitter finality. At 9:30 that night, I threw a blanket at him and told him to get out.

The Unraveling

That was where fourteen years began to unravel. A single *yes* in a kitchen in Indiana produced a cascade: a couch, an ultimatum enforced, a ten-hour drive of pretending, an admission that made the rest of our life untenable.

I remember the sensation of the house after he left. The rooms that had been two people's faded into my responsibility and my sons' needs. The boys handled it with a kind of numb bravery that made me both proud and furious. Bedtimes became practical. Conversations had to be measured. There was grief in the small things: the empty side of the bed, the unpaid bills that reappeared like old creditors, the way a backyard chore suddenly had to be split differently.

There was also a clarity. The question that my friend asked and the answer Josh gave were a gift in the shape of a wound. They forced a decision that had been gnawing at me—stay and erode into silence or leave and try to build something safer for my boys. I chose the latter. The night I threw the blanket, he left. The next morning, the work of disentangling began.

FOURTEEN
TWENTY-TWO

The Call from Tony

"Hailey." Tony's voice was low and steady, but each syllable hit like a weight. "I don't mean to alarm you, but you need to get to the doctor. Tomorrow morning. Get tested for every STD, including HIV."

The kitchen tilted. The refrigerator hummed too loud. I put the phone to my ear and could not move. Tony was our marriage counselor. We had come to him to patch us up, to find one small stitch of hope. Instead, the truth had poured out of Josh in his office, blunt and dark enough that Tony, who had sat with couples through every imaginable wound, sounded shaken on the line.

"Josh just confessed," Tony said. "It is worse than you think. What he told me, I cannot repeat. There are things he has done I will never unsee."

The words splintered me. My hands trembled. Breathing became a work I had to remember how to do.

The Waiting Room

The urgent care facility smelled of antiseptic and old coffee. A fish tank bubbled, a pale distraction. Magazines lay fanned and face down. I sat watching a paper cup deepen with my cold tea and listened to HIV ring through my head like a drum.

When the nurse called my name, I walked down the hall as if someone else had borrowed my body. The exam room was small and bright. Paper crinkled when I climbed onto the table. The nurse closed the door gently, then asked, "So what brings you in today?"

"My husband," I said. The word scraped. "He has been unfaithful. I need to be tested for everything."

She moved with professional softness. Gown. Swabs. Blood vials labeled with neat stickers. Each needle prick felt like a verdict handed down in a language I could not translate. They ran panels I had never imagined. The HIV result would take months because the virus can hide. That waiting lived like barbed wire around my throat.

When the cuff squeezed my arm, the monitor flashed 138 over 78. My body registered numbers the way it registered betrayal. At twenty-four, I had been healthy, strong, and unbreakable—until I chose breast implants. That decision marked the beginning of my downward spiral in health. Now I was rail-thin and brittle, down to ninety-five pounds. My hair thinned. Sleep had stopped visiting.

The Number

Tony's words came back, bigger and clearer. Then the rest of the confession fell into place.

Twenty-two.

Twenty-two. Sexual affairs. Not rumor. Not a cruel exaggeration. Josh told me himself.

The list that followed was savage and specific.

There were prostitutes.

There were men.

There was a fifteen-year-old girl from our church.

There was an orgy.

Even a neighbor I had once considered a friend.

Each item landed like a blow, precise and impossible to soften.

I stared at my hands as if contamination might be visible on skin. My wedding ring, once a steady circle, burned like a shackle. Twenty-two was not a number. It was a sentence. It closed a door with a clang I could not ignore.

Paper and Consequence

I wanted to scream, to tear the house apart, to burn the things that smelled like him. Instead, I did a harder thing. I put words on a screen and sent them into the rooms where people expected us to be whole.

Our Indiana friends—the same ones who had asked the question in their kitchen—were now sitting on the board of directors for Josh's golf ministry. They had no idea. They had no sense of the private arc of betrayal that one seemingly harmless question had set loose. That fact made me angrier in a clean, cold way. Their astonished faces would come later.

For now, I had to turn my grief into a written account—not for healing, but to document the egregious pattern of betrayal for the judge.

I sat at the computer with fingers that would not steady and wrote the most excruciating email I have ever sent.

Email to Joe L., Board Chair

August 20, 2010

Joe,

The boys and I are hanging in there. It has been a rough time. I was shocked and deeply hurt by what I learned about Josh. Since July 24 he has confessed to multiple affairs. At least twenty two sexual affairs and many more emotional betrayals. After fourteen years together I discovered he has been living a double life.

My counselor insists I leave out graphic details for the boys' sake. They know their father has been unfaithful several times and that I forgave him before. This time it has gone too far for reconciliation.

The stress has taken a serious toll on my health. I am nauseous most days, losing weight and hair, and cannot sleep even with medication. My blood pressure spiked to 138 over 78. Two weeks ago Tony urged me to get tested for STDs because of Josh's risky behavior. So far the tests are clear, but HIV can remain dormant. I will be retested at three and six months.

On July 24, at my request, Josh moved out and is staying with a friend. I have filed for divorce and Tony strongly supports that decision. The boys are aware in a general sense. They are angry, but they understand why I cannot allow this to continue. Healing will be long.

I am also dealing with the financial reality. Our monthly bills are roughly $5,800 and Josh has provided $1,300 since July 24. Medical bills drained our savings. I am working toward an associate's degree, and I am limited in how much work I can take on given my health and the boys' needs.

Through it all I am clinging to God. I ask for your prayers for healing, wisdom, and strength. Thank you for your support.

Blessings,

Hailey

Aftermath

That night, the house felt too loud and too empty. The boys moved through routines like ghosts wearing familiar clothes. They put on their headphones and pretended the playlist could shield them. I watched them in the hallway mirror and felt a fierce, practical love. Bedtime became small triage. Breakfasts became appointments. Laundry and math homework and doctor calls were the new liturgy.

The Board of Directors of our ministry would get the email, and then the meeting would ripple out. People who had sat across our table and laughed had no clue of the ledger I was now carrying. That shocked me in a way that sharpened action into necessity.

I folded the laptop closed and pressed my forehead to the wood of the table until the room stopped spinning. The work had begun. Evidence, tests, legal papers, custody conversations, financial lists. The life we had built together unspooled into a long list of items to manage and survive.

Twenty-two. A number, a sentence. A turning point I could not unhear.

FIFTEEN

THE LETTERS HE SENT

Shaping the Story

The night Josh confessed, words came out of his mouth like debris spilling from a wreck. I heard what he admitted, but I also heard what was missing: full truth, accountability, and ownership.

In the days that followed, he began shaping the story himself. He wrote first to the board of his golf ministry, then to my parents, and finally to me. Each letter tried to frame the damage in his own terms. He wanted prayer, forgiveness, covering. What I read was something different: performance, strategy, a man trying to control the narrative even as it collapsed.

These are the words he sent. And this is what they revealed.

To the Board

_____

July 29, 2010

"With tears streaming, I fall on my face before all of you, my friends and brothers, asking for your prayers and forgiveness. I have not been an honest man. I cloaked a vile lifestyle behind a façade of lies and deception. I have crushed the people who mean the most to me... Please cover my wife and children with the blood of Jesus and protect them from the fiery arrows of Satan. I am not able to protect them right now and we are under attack."

Narrator note: His tone was urgent, spiritual, and dramatic. To the board, it sounded like a broken man reaching for redemption. To me, it was a calculated first move. He reached them before I did. His words reached their inboxes before I could send my truth.

To My Parents

July 30, 2010

"You trusted me with Hailey fourteen years ago, and I betrayed that trust. I have caused a hurt so deep it is almost beyond words... I have failed Hailey repeatedly through infidelity. I lived a secret life no one imagined. I am terrified to face you and know your anger would be justified."

Narrator note: He wrote to my parents as though to secure their pity, to cast himself as repentant. He positioned himself not as the perpetrator of destruction but as the prodigal son, sorrowful and afraid. To them, it read as humility. To me, it was another performance.

To Me

August 2, 2010

"How do you begin an apology for crimes so grotesque that I can hardly think about them, let alone put them on paper? ... I have been a sick man from the very beginning. Why the wiring in my head is so broken I do not know... I lay myself before you and ask for your forgiveness. I know I do not deserve it, but I hope in time you may grant it."

Narrator note: This one was for me alone, and it landed like an old ache. His words named grotesque crimes. They carried heavy sorrow. But I had lived through too many cycles of apology followed by relapse. I wanted to believe him. I also knew better.

My Response

On August 19, I wrote to the board. Unlike his letters, mine was not spiritual theater. It was a ledger of facts, a record for the sake of my sons and the court.

"Josh has never come to me with a full confession. I have always found out the hard way—catching him in lies or following a trail that did not fit. Tony, our counselor, has warned me that change is not guaranteed. Narcissism combined with sexual addiction is a powerful, stubborn mix. Add bipolar disorder, compulsive lying, and an eating disorder to the mix, and real recovery will require years of hard work."

"He has confessed to over twenty sexual affairs, including prostitutes, men, orgies, and sex with a minor. The statute of limitations has passed, but the damage to that girl's life was real. She was removed from the worship team, and she has not been the same spiritually since. That should never have happened."

"I genuinely did not know the extent of his life until July 24. Years earlier, there was one affair we thought had been dealt with. A year and a half ago, there were emotional affairs I confronted. I told him then that if he ever did this again, I would leave. Now I am living that consequence."

It was my attempt to set the record straight. His letters had asked for covering. Mine demanded truth.

The Diagnoses I Never Saw Coming

When everything came unglued in 2010, clinicians and counselors began naming what I had lived with for years.

• **Sex addiction.** Josh admitted to twenty-two affairs, including prostitutes, men, an orgy, and even a fifteen-year-old girl from our church. Shouldn't he have been in jail?

• **Bipolar disorder.** The mood swings I could not fix suddenly had context.

• **Narcissistic personality disorder.** One counselor called it the worst case he had ever seen.

• **Bulimia and pathological lying.** Hidden rituals and constant deceit tied everything together.

It was like watching a stranger step out of the man I had married. That stranger was dangerous.

The Cost of His Choices

The cost was not abstract. It was flesh and bone, dollars and bills, grief and shame.

- My body bore the toll of implants I had chosen under his pressure, triggering a cascade of autoimmune symptoms.

- Medical bills devoured savings.
- My boys carried grief they did not deserve.
- Our ministry's reputation collapsed.
- Friends were betrayed.
- And a girl in our church carried scars she never should have borne.

My father said it best in his affidavit to the judge:

"Because of Josh's selfish decisions, [our] family would suffer the consequences for years." He was right. But there was another truth he did not say out loud, one I began to hold inside: *I could survive this. I could protect my boys. I could stop carrying my husband's sins.*

The night I told him to leave, something shifted. I stopped being the wife who covered. I became the woman who would build. That work began immediately—forms, affidavits, doctor appointments, nights of gentle parenting.

It started small. But it started.

SIXTEEN

ONE STORY AWAY

Why the story you are afraid to tell might be the thing that sets you free

I clutched a clipboard with trembling hands in the Department of Social Services waiting room. The fluorescent lights hummed, and one long strip flickered as if it could not be bothered to shine. A toddler's scream rose and fell like a tide. A woman beside me whispered what sounded like a prayer in Spanish, the syllables soft and steady under the noise. The vinyl chair stuck to the back of my legs when I rose, and the clipboard left a dust print on my palm.

I was not supposed to be here.

Months before, I had been the soccer mom who never missed a game, the Bible study leader who could find the right verse for anyone's trouble, the wife who planned anniversary trips and packed lunches with little notes. Now I sat in a government waiting room, filling out forms that asked how I would feed my children next week.

What had brought me here was not a single catastrophe so much as a slow unraveling: a marriage that dissolved under the weight of betrayal, medical bills I could not cover, savings gone in a month, and a daily house full of unanswered questions. I was thirty-one, no degree, no savings, no plan beyond a stubborn hope that we could rebuild.

Humiliation has a texture. It looked like me watching another woman's children through her kitchen window while my own boys practiced soccer in our front yard. It sounded like the cashier asking whether I had enough money for groceries. It felt like the blank stare I gave when a scholarship application asked, "Why do you need financial assistance?"

What I wanted to type was blunt and true: my husband lived a double life and I was the last to know. What I typed instead was small and bureaucratic: our family is in need. Five words that felt like a mask.

That night at the kitchen table, the argument inside me was loud and simple. If I confronted every person I wanted to confront, I might lose the fragile things that remained for my boys. If I stayed silent, we would remain trapped. The choice was not between right and wrong so much as between two kinds of harm. At some point, the choice lit into a hard clarity. Staying silent would become our prison.

Education felt like the lever. I hurried through an associate's degree and took the first steady job I could find. Evenings were for babysitting other people's children and flipping thrift-store finds online. Weekends were for hiding under blankets to build strength for the week. I lost weight until the scale read ninety-three pounds.

Then the scholarship appeared. A women's leadership foundation was offering interviews. They insisted on in-person meetings. The interview was eight hours away. My boss was already unhappy with the time I had to miss for court dates and appointments. I had no paid time off. I had no family nearby to watch the boys. The practicalities read like a wall: miss the interview and stay trapped or miss the job and risk eviction.

I drove to the interview. Night highways have a hard quiet that forces you into a small, serious conversation with yourself.

The room at the foundation smelled of cleaner and coffee. I gripped a three-ring binder in my lap. Inside were receipts and recommendations and a handful of short notes: court dates, late nights, the babysitting shifts that bought a textbook. It was messy and imperfect and honest. Five women sat behind a long table like a small, civilian jury. One of them tapped a pen and asked, tell us what changed for you.

I could have offered a tidy pitch. I did not. I opened the binder and told the truth. Empty fridges. Food stamps. Babysitting other people's children while my own did homework alone. A son's concussion and the long, brittle nights afterward. The shame of a life reduced to survival. Then I described who I wanted to be: a mother with a degree, steady income, the kind of presence that let my sons plan a future instead of counting cans.

Halfway through a paragraph, one woman leaned forward and asked, "How would that change your boys' lives?" I said simply, "It would change everything." Their faces softened. I felt the table tilt in a new direction.

What I did not realize then was that I was already telling a powerful story. I was instinctively doing the four things that would later become the EPIC Framework™, though I had no name for it at the time. I *engaged* those women with an opening that earned the right to be heard. I *persuaded* with concrete details that turned facts into feelings. I *inspired* a larger vision of who my boys and I could become. I *closed* by asking for the single thing that would move everything forward.

For a week the waiting ate at me. Then the phone rang. My stomach did a small, private flip at the out-of-state number. The voice said, "Congratulations, you have been awarded a scholarship."

Five thousand dollars was more than money. It was permission to breathe. That grant opened doors I had thought closed. Telling that one story eventually helped me secure a total of $52,000 in scholarships and grants over the next five years. I finished a bachelor's, then a master's, then an MBA while working full-time and raising my boys.

But the point is not the degrees or the numbers. It is the lesson the interview taught me in the rawest possible terms: truth spoken with precision and structure moves people. Words that are specific, honest, and purposeful have trajectory. They do not fix everything, but they create leverage where there is none.

I did not expect miracles that week. What I got was a chance. The rest I built with long hours, small griefs, and stubborn steps. That one story did not erase the past. It did not close every wound. It gave me a way forward.

You are just one story away from a breakthrough.

What I did in that conference room was not magic; it was structure. If you want the exact, step-by-step playbook that took me from that kitchen table to stages and scholarships, pick up ***EPIC Impact™: Transform Your Message Into a Movement.***

The book walks EPIC through with prompts, templates, and real examples so you can apply it immediately. In a later chapter, I will teach the exact framework that turned rock bottom into rocket fuel.

I will show you EPIC step by step: how to engage your audience, how to persuade with proof, how to inspire a bigger identity, and how to close with clarity. This is not a formula for polished content alone. It is the structure that can transform a message into a movement.

For hands-on help, check out the upcoming companion app at epicimpact.ai—it bundles the same templates and AI-powered prompts from the book into workflows you can use on your phone or laptop.

Visit <u>epicimpact.com</u> or scan the QR code to purchase *EPIC Impact*™ or register for a free live demo.

See how the framework works in real time—and how it can help you craft stories that move people.

Scan me!

SEVENTEEN
EMOTIONAL WHIPLASH

The Night Alex Broke

There had been no warning for the boys. Nothing dramatic had happened in front of them. No yelling, no slamming doors, no raised voices that might have prepared them for the collapse. At home, their father was warm and charming, though he was often distracted. He spent long stretches on his phone or at the computer, physically present but emotionally elsewhere. All they heard from him were words of love, expressing how much he loved them and how much he loved me. That ordinary calm meant the revelation of his double life hit like a truck. It was whiplash: one minute we were a happy family, the next everything was ripped away.

Later, I realized those declarations of pride—"I have the best wife, I have the best kids"—were not for us but for an audience. He said them to impress his friends, to brag about what he had, not to steady the life he was unraveling.

Our counselor later told me that middle school age is the worst time for a divorce. He explained it plainly. Kids that age are building their sense of self. They are testing boundaries, learning what is normal, and watching their peers to figure out who they will become. Trust is a primary currency. When a parent falls from a pedestal, the shock is not only emotional, it is existential. They do not just lose a parent's reliability; they lose a map for who they are. Shame spreads fast. Peer cruelty can turn curiosity into rumor. Grades fall. Friend groups fracture. Anger and rebellion are common responses because middle schoolers often lack the tools to process betrayal. They feel the break in a way that is both sudden and corrosive.

After weeks of showing little emotion, Alex stormed into my room sobbing. His whole body shook as he collapsed onto my bed.

"I just can't take it anymore," he cried. "Why did Dad have to do this to our family?"

His words sliced through me. Andrew stood in the doorway, silent but watchful, his shoulders hunched, sadness written all over him.

Andrew had always been the one who talked, who tried to name whatever hurt him. Alex held things inside, but that night the dam broke. Both boys were trying to make sense of the same impossible irony: their dad, the man they had put on a pedestal, the man who preached faith and integrity, had been living a double life. The image they had carried of him had cracked in half.

Even then, their hearts leaned toward forgiveness. They wanted to understand. They wanted to move forward. They told me they forgave him.

Forgiveness did not erase the wound. It did not remove the confusion of watching their father fall. It did not stop the silent anger curling inside them.

Anchors and Aisles

Despite everything, the boys handled themselves with a strength that surprised me. Earlier that spring, Alex had asked Jesus into his heart and wanted to be baptized. The boys decided they wanted to do it together. On October 10, 2010, they were baptized in front of our church. Josh and I sat on opposite sides of the viewing area, each of us supporting them in our own way, while the congregation watched. By then, my mother had arrived to spend three months with us, helping me as I resumed my college courses. Her presence steadied the household in a small, practical way.

We still looked for every normal rhythm we could keep. Soccer tournaments that had once been routine became lifelines. Finances made everything harder, but I could not imagine the boys missing practices or friends. Those fields were where they could be boys and not have to carry the grown-up problems we were drowning in.

Right before our family imploded, we had adopted two golden retriever puppies. They were a handful, but our counselor encouraged me to keep them for as long as possible, for the sake of routine and comfort. I agreed on one condition: Josh would help cover the vet bills. At first, it felt like one more ordinary, silly thing to anchor us. Then one of the puppies was diagnosed with juvenile cataracts and required care we could not manage. We found him a loving home that could provide for his needs. The boys understood the decision and helped find him the right place.

The first holidays apart were brutal and unfamiliar. What made one December moment unbearable arrived in a place I would never have expected. My parents were visiting, and we were sitting in the large church sanctuary. The aisle split the rows of chairs, and the light poured in high and white. Josh walked in holding the hand of a beautiful blonde bombshell, with the boys following right behind. I was stunned. Not only had he ignored the quiet rule about dating in front of our children, he had no sense of how this would land on them or on me. The boys said they liked her. Their words cut me in a way I did not expect. They were trying to be brave, to be loyal, to make peace with the scattered pieces of their lives.

Wind Turbine Car

One significant boost to Andrew's self-confidence came that spring. My son has always been brilliant in math and science. Even as a middle schooler, his mind worked differently—always tinkering, always solving, always imagining what could be built. In 2011, that brilliance was recognized on a bigger stage: out of nearly 1,500 student inventors from across Greenville, Spartanburg, and Anderson counties, Andrew's creation—a wind turbine car—took top honors at the BI-LO Invention Convention. He was named **Grand Champion of the entire competition**, awarded the **Research and Development Award**, and walked away with a **$1,000 scholarship**. But what mattered more than the medals or money was the pride in his eyes. At just thirteen, he was already proving he could hold his own among the brightest young innovators in the state.

He had a wonderful eighth-grade teacher who noticed what I, as his mother, already knew—Andrew was struggling with self-esteem. She saw beyond his quiet doubts and into his sharp, curious mind. Because of his excellent grades and interest in engineering, she guided him toward the Career and Technology Center for our school district, where he could get hands-on learning that lit him up. If it hadn't been for her intervention—helping him build the wind turbine car and getting him registered for the competition—Andrew might have slipped through the cracks. Instead, this life event became an anchor at precisely the right time, steadying him and showing him who he could be.

For a moment, it felt like we had turned a corner. Andrew was thriving, and I clung to the hope that maybe, just maybe, the boys could rise above the chaos their father had left in his wake. Watching him hold that trophy and scholarship check, I thought perhaps we were finally catching a breath of stability.

But peace has a way of being short-lived in our story. As if Josh had not already made our lives difficult enough, nothing could have prepared me for what was to come next.

EIGHTEEN

THE PAPER TRAIL OF CONTROL

The Spiral

One year after we separated, Josh remarried. He and his girlfriend had been living together for months and had coached the boys to lie to me about it. That betrayal cut deeper than the infidelities had. It was not only that he had a new life; it was that he taught our sons to hide it from their mother.

The house they built after the wedding wasn't just bigger—it was excessive, a showpiece more than a home. With sprawling square footage for two adults, her one daughter, who lived there only part-time, and our boys just three nights a week, it felt less like necessity and more like performance, a structure built to prove something rather than to shelter someone. It cost more than double what our home cost.

To me, it stood as a monument to everything I no longer had. While I clawed for survival on food stamps and Medicaid and pieced together every side hustle I could find, he posted pictures of a new wife and a new life as if we had been disposable. He paraded her at public events and online like proof he had won.

But the glossy surface of his new life did not hide the chaos beneath. I had to take him back to court for contempt not once, not twice, but sixteen times for failure to pay child support and alimony. Sixteen times I sat in stiff courtroom chairs, hands folded in my lap, praying a judge would enforce what was already written in black and white. Each hearing cost me time I did not have. I was paid hourly. Every hour I spent at the courthouse, every trip to meet a lawyer or prepare affidavits, was one less hour I could trade for groceries, utilities, medical care, or the supplements the boys needed.

The energy this fight drained from my classes and my job was more than exhausting. I learned to calculate loss in a new currency: missed wages, missed study time, missed nights. Where once my calendar had held scholarship deadlines and exams, it now held hearings and motions. The legal grind demanded receipts, evidence, and stamina. I turned outrage into paperwork because paperwork, however imperfect, could buy soccer cleats and keep the lights on.

The emails and voicemails were worse than dollars. They came from Josh, wrapped in the language of concern but laced with control. A voicemail might begin, "I am worried about the boys," but it would end with a demand—he would only pay for certain things if he got to choose them.

When Alex needed braces, Josh insisted on an orthodontist forty-five minutes away, even though a perfectly qualified one was just five minutes from the boys' school. The choice was convenient for him but made no sense—especially since he never took Alex to an appointment. I was the one in a gas-guzzling vehicle, rearranging carpool and burning through time and money, while he called it "being involved."

An email would open with, "I just want what is best for the boys," and then unravel into a list of conditions meant to punish and exhaust. The line between caring and control blurred until I could no longer tell where one stopped and the other began. He posted public proclamations of pride and faith while privately using words to bend our lives into his shape.

Sometimes the simplest things exposed the gulf. I found a social post of him smiling at a banquet while an unpaid invoice for Andrew's travel soccer sat in my folder. I filed photos, bank statements, and receipts with clinical care. I wrote affidavits that began, "He still makes decisions that cost my children time, dignity, and opportunity." Typing that line in the dark at two in the morning felt like permission to name the harm that had been nameless for so long.

The spiral was not only legal and financial. It was emotional and moral. My sons carried the public and private contradictions and tried to shield themselves and me. They learned to sign forms and to show up at hearings with more seriousness than their age should allow. They learned that survival sometimes meant telling the truth into a room of strangers and then walking back into a life where the man who had promised to protect them showed up with a new wife and a new address.

We kept fighting because we had to. The court could not fix everything, but it could impose consequences and slow the erosion. The papers kept coming. The hearings kept coming. And with each envelope, we learned another shape of endurance.

Legal Battles That Wouldn't End

In the three years that followed our divorce, I barely recognized how far we had fallen. The envelope was thin and ordinary, the kind of thing the mail should have swallowed and made forgettable. My name was typed neatly on the front. My law firm's return address sat in the corner. My stomach dropped before I tore it open.

I sank into the kitchen chair and unfolded the crisp white paper. Legal language spilled across the page, each line a precise accounting of ways Josh had found to bend or ignore the divorce decree. The list read like a catalog of everyday betrayals:

- Not paying his half of the boys' extracurricular fees.
- Skipping the disability insurance he was court ordered to carry.
- Late alimony. Again.
- Letting one of the boys watch an R rated movie.
- Ignoring the church requirement we had agreed upon.
- Refusing to give me the boys when he was gone for hours at a time.
- Not providing nutritional supplements we had agreed were necessary.

One line stopped me cold and hovered on the page like a command:

"Your communications are inappropriate. They have no legitimate purpose and must stop."

My lawyer's voice echoed in my head as I read: If he does not comply, we will pursue contempt.

That should have been a warning to him. For me it felt like another weight pressing into my chest. Paper threats rarely changed him. He did not think rules applied to him.

Turning Grief into Affidavits

The first hearings were small, crowded, and unbearable. Each of our mothers sat behind us, women who once shared holiday tables and grandchildren now reduced to quiet opponents across a narrow aisle.

What else could they do but take sides? In a courtroom that small, it was impossible not to lock eyes—a reminder that divorce doesn't just split two people, it fractures an entire family.

I remember one hearing in particular. I sat at the worn wooden table, reading Josh's affidavit, my hands shaking as I traced words I knew were false. His attorney had drafted the statement, page after page, not to tell the truth but to distort it. One line in particular caught in my throat: that I had never held a "real job."

The audacity of it made me want to stand up and shout. How could I? I married young. I raised our boys without childcare. I tried to piece together college between thirteen moves Josh forced on us, all while fighting back-to-back health crises that left me scrambling just to function. It wasn't neglect. It was survival.

But the courtroom demanded composure. So I swallowed the scream rising in my chest, kept my face calm, and turned another page. My stomach churned, but I read on, because the record demanded it.

Then something unexpected happened. Josh's mother—a woman of strong character who had once been my ally—refused to endorse certain drafts. She would not put her name to words that cast me in a false light. For a fleeting moment, in the middle of all that legal combat, I saw her not as "his mother," but as a woman unwilling to lie. And if even she could not stomach the story being spun, maybe the truth still had power.

Meanwhile, survival bled into numbers. Every missed payment cut deeper. Late alimony forced me to choose which bill to let slide. The math of survival became a ledger of losses: embarrassed boys, awkward conversations with coaches, doors closing for lack of funds.

Lawyering up felt like learning a new language. My first affidavit was both humiliating and clarifying at once—bank statements, unpaid fees, and broken promises were turned into exhibits.

Some nights, my anger burned reckless. I pictured shooting his tires before reality reminded me I could lose my job. Other nights, I bargained with God, asking why Josh hadn't been taken before the truth surfaced. The thoughts shocked me, but they were real.

In court, I always showed up. He often didn't. Bench warrants were issued, but they were little more than threats. Each absence cost me work hours, classes, and time I could never get back.

The process taught me to treat grief like a task list. I labeled folders, saved voicemails, and boxed pain into evidence. The courts handed down orders, but they couldn't return the hours stolen from my boys or erase the shame they carried.

Still, I kept showing up. If turning grief into exhibits meant keeping my sons fed and with some measure of dignity, then I would do it. File by file, hearing by hearing, endurance became survival.

How the Boys Carried It

Even as I turned grief into affidavits and learned the rhythms of court, the real cost was not only legal or financial. The hearings named his failures, but they could not stop the private work he did to shape how the boys saw him and saw me. Paper could force payment for a month, but it could not erase the quiet whispers, the selective stories, the sideways comments that made a different truth stick inside two growing boys.

Slowly, the battle bled into the house. The more I fought to hold our lives together on paper, the harder he worked to polish his image for everyone else. He apologized in public and rewrote history in private. He painted himself as the wounded party and taught our sons to do the same. At school, at church, in casual conversations with other parents, the version of their father that the boys encountered was the smiling, faithful man he wanted the world to see.

That pressure landed unevenly. Andrew, who had always tried to name his feelings, began to harden. He defended his father fiercely, sometimes with words and sometimes with a fury that flipped on like a switch. At times his anger felt animalistic, startling in its intensity. I did not see it coming. The rage was like an inferno. I did not understand that his allegiance to his father would turn into a blade he sometimes aimed at me.

If I thought the legal battles were exhausting, parenting two out-of-control teenage boys was the hell I never saw coming. Their rebellion was sharp, messy, and relentless. It would take everything I had to try to steady them and keep our family from splintering further.

NINETEEN

FRAGILE HOPES AND FRACTURED NIGHTS

A Mother's Plea for Help

Subject: Request for Urgent Counseling — Andrew

(March 15, 2013)

Tony,

How are you? I need your help. I just learned that Andrew has been experimenting with drugs and alcohol and that he has been driving the car Josh bought him at speeds up to 110 mph. I also discovered a text exchange in which he and a girl were making plans for intimacy. In response I have taken his phone and revoked his driving privileges indefinitely.

He told me he has been trying to numb the pain from the divorce and said he would not care if his car crashed because he does not want to live anymore. That terrified me. Andrew had briefly stopped taking Zoloft, and last week he resumed it because he was hurting so much. He did not want to go back on it, but it is the only thing I know that helps his depression for now.

I would like Andrew to begin seeing you regularly, if you are available and if Josh will agree. Andrew resists counseling but I plan to make regular sessions a condition for returning any priv- ileges. He normally has high school soccer practice after school until 5:30 and sometimes has evening games during the week. I can adjust his schedule to make appointments if you let me know your availability.

This feels urgent. I want a safe plan for him and support for me as I try to parent through this. Please let me know when you can meet with him and any intake steps I should take.

Thank you,

Hailey

Living with a Volcano

Andrew's volatility terrified Alex and me. There were nights I hid my gun and locked my bedroom door because I feared Andrew could fly off the handle. I had to physically restrain him more than once to stop him from hurting Alex; on one occasion, he threw a blunt object at close range, and Alex was shaking with fear. The boys come home from their weekends with Josh different—angrier, colder—and I began to see that whatever was said to them while they were away was shifting how they treated me. I was mother and witness and guardian all at once, and I was scared that without help, this would get worse.

A Spark of Hope

April 15, 2013 – 8:00 a.m.

My phone buzzed with a message from Andrew. I expected something small, maybe about practice or lunch money. Instead, it opened
like a confession.

---

*"Hey Mom, it's Andrew. I've got a temporary emergency phone
case. If you need me, I just want you to know I love you and I'm
sorry for all the wrong things I've done. I've been disrespectful
and haven't let you be the parent while I've been the son. I'm
sorry. Hope to see you tonight. Love you, Mom."*

I read the words twice, my chest tightening. Apologies from him
didn't usually come like this— unprompted, tender, almost trembling
on the edge of manhood and boyhood.

I typed back quickly, fingers shaky but heart steady.

---

*"Hi, honey. It's so good to hear from you. Thank you. I forgive
you and love you very much. I can't wait to see you at your
game tonight. Have a great day."*

I wanted to wrap him in my arms right then, but for now, these words
would have to do.

April 19, 2013 – 6:09 p.m.

Four days later, another message lit up my phone. This one was
longer, more deliberate—as if he'd been carrying the weight of these
words all week.

"Hey Mom. I just want to apologize for the way I have acted. For months I've focused too much on the negative and not the positive. You are my mother. You've cared for me since I was born. You'd do anything for me. You are the best mother in the world, and I wouldn't trade you for anyone else. I've taken advantage of all you do. I'm sorry I didn't turn out to be the son you wanted, but none of my actions are your fault. I want you in my life more than you think. You're the most important person in the world to me. I want our relationship to last and be rock solid. I love you so much, and I know you love me. I look forward to rebuilding what we had three years ago. It'll take time, but I want us back. I'm sorry for everything wrong I've done. I love you."

His words were clumsy in places, but they carried a raw sincerity no polished letter could. He was trying. He wanted me.

I responded simply, afraid that if I said too much, I'd smother the fragile spark of hope he was offering.

"Ok. Thank you for your kind words. I love you very much and look forward to restoring our relationship."

I set my phone down and sobbed until my whole body shook. Was God finally answering my prayers and returning my sweet, wayward child? For the first time in so long, I felt the possibility of repair. His words were unpolished, but they dripped with sincerity. He was reaching for me. He was reaching for home.

But even as I wiped my tears and tucked that message away in my heart, life had other plans. Change was never linear with Andrew. Hope would rise, only to be shattered by the next reckless choice.

And just days later, in the dead of night, I was jolted awake by a sound that would remind me how fragile that hope truly was.

TWENTY

FIRECRACKERS AND FREEFALLS

Andrew and Luke's Wild Ride

Bang, Bang, Bang

It was the night before Alex's fourteenth birthday party. June 2013.

Bang. Bang. Bang.

I jolted awake. The alarm read 3:00 a.m. At first, I thought I was dreaming, but then I heard it again— loud, urgent banging at the front door. I looked out the window and saw a car in my driveway. I didn't recognize it. My heart was pounding.

I rushed to the door and opened it. A furious man stood there, demanding, *"Where are the boys who were driving that car?"* He pointed to the vehicle—it was my son's friend Luke's car.

I said, *"They're sleeping right here in the living room,"* and pointed toward the couch.

He shook his head. *"Oh no, they're not sleeping!"*

That's when the truth came pouring out. Andrew and Luke had snuck out in the middle of the night and taken Luke's car for a joyride. At some point, Andrew, sitting in the passenger seat, thought it would be funny to light a firecracker and throw it out the window.

Bad idea.

They caught the attention of an undercover police officer who began tailing them. Instead of pulling over, the boys hit the gas.

They tore through backroads, flying around corners on loose gravel. The officer said they nearly lost control several times. Eventually, they got back on the freeway and pushed the car to 120 miles per hour. When they finally thought they'd lost the cop, they pulled over, switched drivers, and Andrew drove them home as if nothing had happened.

I invited the officer into my home. Not long after, Luke's parents arrived. We all sat in the living room while the officer—clearly furious, and rightly so—berated the boys. His voice echoed through the house.

I asked, "Are you going to arrest them?"

Honestly, I hoped the answer would be yes. Deep down, I believed it might be the wake-up call they both desperately needed. But instead of consequences, there were excuses.

Luke's parents pleaded with the officer not to press charges. I stood there stunned, waiting for accountability—and instead, I got blamed.

 As they walked out the door with their son, Luke's mother turned to me and said, "You must have known what they were doing. How could you let this happen?"

Her comment enraged me: no one had ever questioned my parenting before. And if she had any idea what I was up against—a father doing everything he could to unravel what I tried to build—she might have understood. Instead, I was left speechless.

What made it cut even deeper was that I had considered her a friend. We had shared stories about our sons over lunch, swapped parenting advice, and she had even invited me to join her women's Bible study group. Her words that day didn't come from a stranger—they came from someone I trusted.

What shook me even more, though, were Andrew's excuses. The way he defended Luke—downplaying, rationalizing, brushing past what had happened—felt like déjà vu. It was the same pattern I had lived through with Josh: charm, denial, and avoidance dressed up as reason. The echo was chilling. For the first time, I wondered if Andrew might become him—and that thought alone was my worst nightmare.

I stood in the wreckage of that moment—humiliated, heartbroken, and more determined than ever to draw a hard line with my son.

I turned to Andrew and said, *"Give me your license."*

He handed it over. I gave it to the officer and said, *"Hold on to this until I figure out what his punishment will be."*

That was on a Friday.

Mom Took the Keys, Not the Excuses

On Monday, I went down to the station, picked up Andrew's driver's license, and drove straight to the DMV. I walked up to the counter and told the clerk, "I am surrendering this license. I will not be responsible for my son killing himself or someone else."

The clerk looked at me in disbelief.

She said, "No parent has ever done this before."

I stood firm. I wasn't there to be liked. I was there to save my son's life.

But instead of support, I got undermined.

Jos went behind my back three weeks later and got Andrew's license reinstated.

Just like that, the consequences I'd fought so hard to enforce were erased. And the destructive behavior continued.

It was like trying to swim upstream in a river of chaos. I was fighting to discipline Andrew in a way that could correct him. Josh was fighting me in the opposite direction, undoing everything I had done.

Consequences Versus Convenience — June 28, 2013

I warned Josh that Andrew's driving was no longer about teenage recklessness; it was a matter of life and death. After Alex told me he was scared to ride with both Andrew and Josh, and even his best friend's mother refused to let her son ride with Josh anymore, I knew the problem ran deeper than impulsivity. It was learned behavior: recklessness without accountability.

I placed a tracking device on Andrew's car and discovered speeds up to 120 miles per hour, sometimes while he was under the influence. Despite warnings from his psychiatrist, Dr. Buford, and clear evidence of danger, Josh continued to return the car and failed to monitor him as promised.

When the boys fled that night, they reached 120 miles per hour again. Officer G. later said he could not believe they survived and warned that if Andrew caused a crash, I could face criminal or civil charges because I had signed for his license.

I had already scheduled an evaluation with Dr. Fisher at an adolescent psychiatric clinic and begged Josh to suspend Andrew's driving until he was cleared. My message was simple: **Andrew did not**

need convenience; he needed consequences. What terrified me most was realizing he was learning from the one person who should have been teaching him better.

The Broken Promise and The Breakthrough

Josh hired Andrew for summer construction work and promised him $6,000 in pay. But like so many of his promises, it dissolved into disappointment. When the summer ended, instead of a paycheck, Josh tossed him a junk car worth barely $2,000.

"You've already been paid," he told him flatly. "That car is your payment."

It wasn't just about the money. It was about trust. It was another moment that told Andrew, once again, that his father's word could not be counted on. I saw it in his face—the disbelief first, then the quiet ache that settled behind his eyes.

That summer had already been bruising in every way. The emotional damage was matched by the physical. Andrew told me how his dad had slammed the toolbox compartment on the truck while his hand was still there. He was certain Josh saw it, yet the lid came down anyway.

In another instance, sunburned from a fishing outing, Andrew said his dad slapped his leg hard enough to leave him in pain for days. Later, during what was supposed to be harmless wrestling, Josh shoved him into a doorframe so forcefully that Andrew's back hurt for weeks.

It infuriated me to see how often Josh crossed the line with Andrew—how he always took it too far with him but never with Alex. The favoritism was unmistakable. The cruelty, unforgivable.

When the truck incident happened, Andrew came home quieter than usual. He didn't rage or cry. He just sat at the table, hands still bruised, staring at them like he was trying to make sense of something that finally couldn't be explained away.

"He didn't even say sorry," he whispered. "He looked right at me."

That moment broke something open. For the first time, Andrew wasn't just hurt—he was awake. He saw who his dad really was, not the version he had hoped for. It devastated him, but it also gave him clarity. The illusion was gone.

At the same time, I could see his impulsive behavior spiraling into something deeper than teenage rebellion. Knowing Josh's history with bipolar disorder and addiction, I could no longer dismiss the warning signs. The thrill-seeking, the recklessness—it wasn't just defiance. His brain was chasing stimulation it couldn't regulate on its own.

I was desperate for answers, and I refused to give up on my sweet boy. That desperation led me to the Amen Clinic in Atlanta. Whatever it cost, whatever it required of me, I was determined to get the answers he needed and the healing he deserved.

TWENTY-ONE

FIGHTING FOR ANSWERS

A Summer of Breaking Points

By the end of that summer, I was worn down to the bone. The joyride, the violence, the anger, the endless phone calls from teachers —I felt like I was running triage in my own home every single day. Andrew's moods swung from high to low within minutes. He would drive recklessly, lash out at me and Alex, and then collapse into despair, saying he didn't want to live anymore. His concussions from soccer only worsened things, and the Zoloft that once helped was no longer enough.

I had tried everything I knew: doctors, counselors, discipline, structure, prayer. Nothing held for long. He was brilliant and broken all at once, and I was exhausted from trying to hold the pieces together.

Finally, a Yes

That summer, for the first time, Andrew agreed to accept help. I don't know if it was exhaustion, desperation, or a flicker of self-awareness, but something inside him softened. After years of fighting me on doctors and counselors, he finally said yes. That one word cracked open a window of hope I hadn't felt in a long time.

The Amen Clinic

I knew exactly where I wanted to take him. Years earlier, his father, Josh, had undergone an evaluation at the Amen Clinic in Seattle. That three-day assessment changed everything for him: for once, there was a name for his illness and a plan for how to manage it. It hadn't erased all of Josh's demons, but it had given us something solid to hold onto in the chaos.

So I called the Amen Clinic in Atlanta, scheduled the evaluation, and paid for it all myself. I didn't care what it cost. I just wanted answers for Andrew.

Three Days in Atlanta

For three days, they evaluated him from every angle—his brain, his history, his behavior, his pain. They ran brain SPECT imaging, psychological assessments, and in-depth interviews. Unlike so many other doctors who had spent twenty minutes with him before sending us home with another prescription, they *looked* at his brain. They dug deeper. They connected the dots.

And at the end of those three days, we finally had clarity. The results confirmed what I had long suspected: Andrew was struggling with a mood disorder and ADHD. Seeing it in black and white, backed by scans and testing, was both heartbreaking and relieving. We finally had a name for the chaos, and with that, a treatment plan that offered real direction.

Putting a Name to the Pain

For so long, I had been battling shadows, trying to protect Andrew without even knowing what enemy I was fighting. Now I had a roadmap. Medication adjustments, therapy approaches, lifestyle changes—it wasn't a magic cure, but it was a foundation. For the first time in years, I felt like we weren't fumbling in the dark.

My Verdict as His Mother

This chapter—this long, weary accounting—is my summary to two psychiatrists. It is my proof of how hard I fought for Andrew. How I wrote letters, made calls, paid bills, drove miles, and sat in sterile waiting rooms because I refused to give up on my son.

I wanted them to know that Andrew was more than his symptoms. He was the boy who once built a wind turbine car and won a scholarship. The boy who captained his soccer team. The boy who had been broken open by life before he had a chance to fully live it.

And I was the mother who carried him through those years of chaos, who did everything in her power to hold the line until we finally had answers.

A Fresh Start

He started medication the week school began. Three weeks later, he walked through the door with a quiet glow in his face and said, *"Mom, today was the first day I felt smart. I could follow along with the teacher. I understood everything."*

His grades improved. His attitude softened. He was coming back to me—the sweet, funny, thoughtful boy I knew had always been there beneath the chaos.

But in our story, peace never seemed to last long.

Everything would unravel again—this time, at the hands of another student.

TWENTY-TWO

A MOTHER'S WAR

October 2, 2013 – The Assault

It started as an ordinary day at high school. It became the day that changed Andrew's life.

In less than ten minutes, Austin—a six-foot, 185-pound baseball player, illegally recruited from Massachusetts—hunted down my son in two separate locations.

First in the parking lot, when he rolled down his window and sneered, "WHAT THE F*** YOU LOOKING AT?"

Andrew, my 5'6", 130-pound boy, didn't respond. He kept walking. But Austin wasn't finished. Minutes later, inside the school, he slammed Andrew into a concrete wall with such force that his head split open.

A one-inch gash. Two staples. A severe concussion—his fourth. Three previous concussions were from soccer.

For three weeks, Andrew couldn't attend school. He sat at home with sunglasses on, nauseated, dizzy, and crying in pain. And while he suffered, Austin got just three days of out-of-school suspension. Three days. Then he conveniently returned to Massachusetts, free to play baseball while my son's future lay in ruins.

October 4, 2013 – The First Rallying Cry

I wasn't the only parent outraged. Kim, whose son Mitchell had also been terrorized by Austin, wrote to the school: "I believe Wednesday is still being considered a fight issue when it was clearly an unprovoked attack by a much larger perpetrator on a smaller victim. If bullying really is an intolerable offense at this school, then it would be a grave and tragic decision not to expel Austin, just as you would if he had carried a weapon onto the school grounds."

She was right. Her son, Mitchell, had received threatening texts for three weeks before the attack. He was so terrified that he dropped a class just to avoid Austin. Yet the school treated it like a scuffle instead of what it was—an assault.

October 30, 2013 – The Vanishing Video

I reached out to the principal, desperate for evidence. The attack had been caught on the school's cameras. I had seen the video myself, as had the assistant principal. It clearly showed Austin hunting my son down.

Her reply cut me in half: "Our camera system only keeps a video for 14 days. The school deals with the situation within that time span. If we had been told by law enforcement/an attorney/etc that the video was needed, we would have provided it for them during that time."

By the time charges reached the Solicitor's Office, the video was gone. Erased.

I fired back in disbelief: "Thanks for the information, although I'm very disappointed. The process of dealing with charges takes much longer than 14 days. DJJ hasn't even gotten the paperwork to the Solicitor's Office, and it's already been four weeks. By the time an attorney or prosecutor would have known about the video, it could be several weeks after the incident. It may be good for the future to hold onto that kind of information longer than 14 days."

With the evidence gone, justice was slipping through my fingers.

November 4–5, 2013 – The First Legal Battle

By the time I reached attorney Pierce, I was running on caffeine and desperation. I laid out everything in a long email: the assault, the erased video, the concussion, the school's indifference, the lack of accountability. My son had been attacked on campus, and the system was protecting the aggressor.

I hit "send," praying someone would finally help us fight back.

His reply came the next morning.

"I believe I would have a conflict of interest if I represented your son," he wrote. "I probably learned facts from my previous conversations that would create a conflict."

I read it twice before it sank in. A conflict of interest. That meant he had already spoken with someone—**the other side.**

The air went out of me. How could this happen? How could an attorney I trusted be off the table before we even had a chance to begin?

I wrote back, pleading with him to reconsider. *"If you can't represent us," I said, "then please—refer me to the second-best attorney you know."*

He replied quickly, but his answer offered no comfort.

"I'm sorry. It would be unethical for me to take this case, even indirectly. I'll try to find you someone else."

Someone else. Another stranger. Another delay. Another closed door.

I sat staring at the email, my hands shaking, the screen blurring through tears. My son had been assaulted. The evidence had vanished. And now, even the justice system was slipping away—one gatekeeper at a time.

February 2014 – The DJJ and the Doctors

By February, Andrew's concussion symptoms still hadn't lifted. I wrote to our legal team, torn between protecting him and not sabotaging his case: "Andrew has not fully recovered from his concussion; however, his doctor released him to play soccer. The soccer coach is requesting a copy of the letter... Are we going to hurt our chances for receiving compensation for Andrew's injury from the school or the other kid's parents if Andrew plays?"

Attorney Blake. replied cautiously: "If the doctor has released him, then it will not hurt our case for him to play unless you believe the doctor's release is premature. The only way the release could hurt our case is that most definitely the potential defense attorney will use it to suggest that Andrew is symptom-free as of the date of the release."

But Andrew wasn't symptom-free. He was still foggy, his thinking slow, words slipping from him. His math and science teachers had to drop him down to lower-level courses. His Spanish teacher refused to submit assignments to the homebound tutor, costing him an entire class and wrecking his GPA.

DJJ was still in the process of tracking down Austin's address so he could be served."

March 2014 – The Long Road

The legal wheels turned slowly.

More waiting. More paperwork. More bills piling up.

For the most part, Andrew's symptoms have subsided, all except the foggy thinking. He feels like things are in slow motion sometimes and is not as 'sharp' as he used to be. He had to drop his Honors courses for the second semester so he could keep up.

The Final Insult

After everything—my son's suffering, months of emails, countless hours at doctors' offices, and a mother's endless fight for justice—what we received was a single piece of paper.

A letter of apology.

But it wasn't even from Austin It was clearly written by his mother, in handwriting and phrasing no teenage boy would ever use.

It was hollow. Pathetic. A slap in the face.

A Mother's Verdict

I fought with everything in me:

- I wrote letters.

- I pressed charges.

- I argued with principals.

- I begged attorneys.

- I documented every symptom, every setback, every injustice.

And still, in the end, there was no justice.

The illegally recruited player, who should never have been at that school, received a three-day suspension and returned to baseball in his home state.

My son, meanwhile, was left with the scars: foggy thinking, lost classes, wrecked confidence, and the fear that he would never be himself again.

And I was left with the guilt of knowing that no matter how hard I fought, I couldn't protect him.

What Future Was Left for Andrew?

This was the same boy who once lit up science fairs and engineering labs—**Grand Champion of the 2011 Bi-Lo Invention Convention**, winner of the **Research and Development Award**, a student at the **Career and Technology Center** where he thrived in engineering courses. He worked part-time at **O'Reilly Auto Parts**, captained his high school soccer team, and dreamed of playing in college. The contrast between who he was then and who he had become was crushing.

For years, I believed his path would lead to becoming an engineer, a future as bright and determined as the boy who built a wind turbine car in eighth grade. But after the assault, those hopes began to slip. At that point, my dream for him had shrunk to something painfully simple: that he would at least graduate high school. What I couldn't admit—not yet, not even to myself—was how close I feared we were to losing even that.

Names and identifying details have been changed to protect the privacy of individuals.

TWENTY-THREE

DEGREES IN THE DARK

Building While Breaking

While Andrew's life was spiraling, I was building mine piece by piece.

2013 – Laying a Foundation

In May of 2013, I graduated with my **associate's degree in health information management** from Greenville Technical College. For years, I had dreamed of advancing my education, but divorce, finances, and raising two boys had always seemed to push that dream further out of reach. Still, I pressed forward, taking night classes, online courses, whatever I could manage.

That summer, I passed my exam and became a **Registered Health Information Technician (RHIT)** — an achievement that felt almost unreal for a single mom running on borrowed energy.

In the fall of 2013, I landed a job at a **psychiatric hospital** that was part of the South Carolina Department of Mental Health. On paper, the pay was terrible. But I took the job for one reason: the manager was willing to support me as I continued my education. As long as I got my work done, I could use the flexibility of my schedule to chip away at my studies. With two boys in school, soccer practices, church commitments, and weekend tournaments, my time was already carved into fragments. This job made it possible for me to stitch those fragments into something meaningful.

The Work

The hospital was unlike any environment I had ever been in. Every chart I coded, every case I reviewed, carried the weight of someone's suffering. I coordinated meetings with multidisciplinary teams, facilitated process improvements, supervised HIM staff, and conducted chart audits. I learned the language of psychiatry through diagnosis codes—but behind every code was a life, a family, a story unraveling.

In one sense, the work gave me skills and credentials. But in another, it gave me perspective. Every day, I touched the paperwork of people whose struggles mirrored my own family's: depression, anxiety, bipolar disorder, addiction. I was living it at home and reading it at work. It was both heavy and strangely affirming.

2013–2014 – Pressing Forward

With steady work under my belt, I turned my focus to continuing my education. I began applying for scholarships everywhere I could find them, usually late at night when the house was finally quiet. Some nights I fell asleep over my laptop, but I refused to stop. I knew education was the only path forward for me and my boys.

In February 2014, I applied for the **Women in Philanthropy and Leadership (WIPL) Endowed Scholarship** at Coastal Carolina University. My essay told the truth of who I was: a single mother of two teenagers, working full-time at a psychiatric hospital, carrying a 3.848 GPA, and determined to finish my bachelor's degree in health administration. I wrote about my service at church, my years leading Mothers of Preschoolers, and my passion for mental health advocacy. I wanted them to know that I wasn't just studying healthcare administration; I was *living* it, both in my work and at home.

On **May 6, 2014**, the letter arrived.

I had been chosen as the **first-ever recipient** of the WIPL Endowed Scholarship.

A Parallel Story

The timing was surreal. While Andrew was slipping further away—his grades collapsing, his moods unpredictable, his recklessness terrifying—I was finding traction in my own life. While I was fighting for him in schools and doctors' offices, I was also fighting for myself in classrooms and applications.

I was invited to donor dinners and scholarship receptions, where I was treated like someone whose persistence mattered. I still remember standing in those rooms, exhausted from the week, but holding my head high as I introduced myself as a scholarship recipient, a single mother, and a future leader in healthcare. In those moments, I began to believe that maybe my life could be rebuilt, even if Andrew's felt like it was unraveling.

The Weight of Both Worlds

Balancing both stories was exhausting. During the day, I sat in meetings with doctors and administrators, reviewing codes and compliance at the psychiatric hospital. At night, I wrote essays and studied for exams. In between, I managed Andrew's counseling appointments, fought with principals, and fielded angry outbursts.

By the end of 2014, the contrast was almost unbearable. My world was expanding with opportunities, recognition, and hope. Andrew's was shrinking under the weight of concussions, anxiety, and rebellion.

And yet, I pressed forward—because for me, moving forward wasn't just about me. It was about showing Andrew and Alex that even in the middle of chaos, their mother refused to quit.

I was resourceful—sometimes too resourceful. What I didn't know then was that the same grit that kept us afloat would soon lead me into a gamble that threatened to drown us all. And it began with what looked like salvation, neatly stacked in the trunk of my car.

TWENTY-FOUR

THE POISON IS THE CURE

The Hustle of Staying Afloat

After the divorce, survival became an endless hustle. I babysat neighbors' children, substitute-taught at my sons' school, and scoured thrift stores, Craigslist, and eBay for anything I could flip. Even if I made only five dollars after an hour of work, it was proof I could keep us alive one more day.

Luxury purses became my specialty. I couldn't afford one for myself, but I could buy a scuffed-up Coach or Gucci, scrub and polish it until it gleamed, and resell it for a small profit. Each sale was a tiny victory, even if it barely covered the cost of gas for the week.

I also rented out the bonus room in our home, but only to women—mostly traveling nurses or students finishing their clinical rotations at local hospitals. The boys and I gave up privacy, sharing bathrooms, the kitchen, even the family TV.

The guest bathroom was right next to my bedroom, and many of the nurses worked third shift. As a light sleeper, I would often wake up to the sound of showers or footsteps in the middle of the night, and then lie there, staring at the ceiling, unable to drift back to sleep. Oh, how I longed for a home that was ours again, quiet and undisturbed. But this was what survival required, and I held on to the hope that one day things would be different.

Often, sharing our space was awkward, but sometimes, renters became friends, and that was a blessing. Friend or not, their every check helped pay the mortgage and keep a roof over our heads. One nurse was a free spirit who liked to hang her freshly washed bras on the branches of our tree to dry in the breeze. Another loved to cook, which drove me crazy since she spent more time in my kitchen than I did.

The boys had to adjust, too. We kept one shelf in the fridge strictly for the renter, which was no small feat, considering Andrew was always prowling for food like a starving wolf. His appetite was legendary—he could put away a dozen eggs a day, six in the morning and six in the evening. Eventually, I had to buy a second fridge for the garage just to keep up with the food demands between my renter and two endlessly hungry boys.

To his credit, Andrew pulled his weight. Once he started working, he paid for his own car insurance, gas, and eating out—and even chipped in for groceries. He was thoughtful like that, and I saw him maturing right before my eyes. Alex, on the other hand, preferred to save his money, perfectly content to let me shoulder the grocery bills. Typical younger brother.

Even with Andrew's help, the strain never lifted. I was constantly doing mental math: juggling finances, patching together side hustles, squeezing in coursework, showing up for work, and still trying to keep my boys from spiraling into trouble. Some nights, I collapsed into bed more tired than I thought possible, my brain still racing over which bill I could delay for one more week.

I wasn't doing it alone. My parents carried us too, even from 2,000 miles away. As an only child, I saw how much they sacrificed for me and their grandsons. Every month, they quietly filled the gaps so the boys could stay in soccer, eat decent meals, wear clothes that fit, and occasionally enjoy a dinner out. They delayed their own retirement, set aside their cherished dream of building a cabin, and poured those resources into keeping us afloat. My mother's prayers and steady support were the lifeline that steadied me when my own strength ran out.

So when I found a dealer willing to sell me popular exercise DVD sets at wholesale, it felt like striking gold. For a brief, heady moment, I believed I had cracked the code—finally found a way to climb out of scarcity.

For eight weeks, the DVDs sold like wildfire on eBay. Even the mail carrier cheered me on, gladly loading fifty packages at a time. I couldn't believe it. After years of scraping together five-dollar profits from handbags and thrift store finds, I thought I had finally stumbled into stability.

Then came December 2014. I had just spent $3,000 on my biggest order yet. The boxes were still in the trunk of my car when I pulled a letter from the mailbox.

A major fitness company had come after me. Cease-and-desist. Federal lawsuit. Damages. Words like "counterfeit" and "infringement" jumped off the page. They demanded $15,000 in settlement—money I didn't have and couldn't dream of finding.

I sat shaking, realizing I had gambled everything on a hustle that could cost me more than I'd ever earned. I hadn't known the DVDs were counterfeit, pirated copies disguised as the real thing. To Beachbody's lawyers, none of that mattered. To them, I was just another infringer in their crosshairs.

Thankfully, after tense negotiations, I was able to settle for a smaller amount. But the inventory in my trunk was worthless. Trash. The wholesaler vanished, never to be found. And my "gold mine" had become another crushing blow.

I had gone from polishing used handbags for gas money to staring down the threat of federal court. I wasn't afraid of starting over anymore. What scared me was realizing how easily everything I was building for them could vanish overnight. I thought I'd faced every kind of collapse, but nothing prepares you for watching your child break and being powerless to stop it.

TWENTY-FIVE

MY STEADY ONE

"Mini-Me"

If Andrew was my storm, Alex was my steady ground. He was just two years younger, but in so many ways he felt older, calmer, wiser. He was most like me, same personality type (INTJ), and that meant we thought alike, processed alike, and found comfort in structure. Where Andrew often had a skewed view of events, Alex saw things plainly and logically. That bond made him my "mama's boy," though only for a season. As he grew into himself, he yearned for independence, but during those years, we shared a closeness that sustained me.

Discipline and Drive

From early on, Alex excelled in the classroom. His grades earned him a place in the **National Honor Society** and **Beta Club**. He was consistently on the **Principal's List** or **A/B Honor Roll**, and he pushed himself with a schedule full of **Honors, AP, and dual-credit courses**.

By 2014, he was already enrolled in a biomedical science course at the district's Career and Technology Center, exploring an interest in medicine. The following year, he would take four dual-credit college courses while still in high school.

His academic performance also opened doors outside of school. He volunteered at **our hospital** in a two-week summer program, shadowed professionals at the **physical therapy field**, and gave his time to service at church and homeless shelter. Everywhere he went, Alex carried himself with the same quiet discipline that marked his studies.

Leadership on the Field

If academics showed his discipline, soccer revealed his heart. Alex had played since he was four, and by his teen years, his talent and leadership stood out.

- At 12, he set his team's **juggling record**, keeping the ball in the air hundreds of times without letting it touch the ground.
- At 13, he captained his club team to a **state championship**, then led them into regional play.
- By 15, he earned a spot on the **state's top-level competitive team**, one that only accepted the best players.
- He was named **captain** repeatedly on both club and school teams.
- As a junior, his peers chose him as **Varsity Captain** for his high school team, a role that showed not only his skill but the respect he commanded.
- In tournaments, he earned multiple **VIP awards** and recognition as a **top goal scorer**.

Soccer wasn't just a sport for Alex; it was a proving ground for leadership. He had a way of pulling a team together when it mattered most.

The Cost of Opportunities

Alex had the skill to try out for the **Olympic Development Program (ODP)**, a national pathway for elite players, but I couldn't make it happen. As a single mom working full-time while attending college, the money and time required were more than I had. The practices were two hours away. I wrestled with guilt over that, but Alex rarely complained. He made the most of every opportunity that was within reach.

A Natural Leader

What stood out most about Alex wasn't just his GPA or his goals. It was his character. He was responsible, hardworking, and respectful. Teachers and coaches noticed. He volunteered consistently: serving Thanksgiving meals at a homeless shelter, greeting at our church, and stepping into leadership roles with his youth group.

In every sphere—school, sports, church—Alex's quiet influence rippled outward. He didn't need to be the loudest voice; he led by example.

Setback in Spring 2014

Just as Alex was hitting his stride academically and athletically, life threw us another challenge. In the spring of 2014, during one of the last junior varsity soccer games of the season, Alex broke both bones in his left arm at the wrist. I was in the bleachers when a player made an illegal move, and Alex fell backward. He let out a scream that sounded like a wounded animal dying. I rushed to the field and saw immediately that his arm was broken.

We had a 40-minute drive to the ER, and I had to help prop his arm up because if it shifted even slightly, he writhed in pain. With my other hand, I stroked his hair and tried to console him. When I removed my hand to try and steer, he begged me to put it back on his head. Driving with one hand—and sometimes my knee—was challenging, but it was the only way to get him there.

Once inside the ER, as the sedation set in, Alex transformed. He turned into a comedian and a Casanova rolled into one. He told the nurses he was a "baller," compared himself to Lionel Messi, and announced he was going to start his own soccer network. He marveled at the hospital lights, saying they lit up the whole room "vividly," and then, out of nowhere, launched into a ramble about *Red Dawn*, Carfax, and stolen Toyota Camrys. When a nurse told him to relax, he shot back, "I don't like to relax. I like the facts." Even in the middle of pain and chaos, his humor and personality spilled out in a way that made us laugh through the fear.

The ER doctor initially set the arm, but at our follow-up with the orthopedic surgeon, we learned it hadn't been done properly. By then, the bone had already started to heal, and the surgeon had to reset it. He gave Alex only a shot of numbing medication, no sedation. It was incredibly painful for him, and almost unbearable for me to watch. It felt like child abuse that they didn't schedule a proper procedure under anesthesia. Alex screamed and cursed at the orthopedic surgeon in a way I didn't know was in him. I wanted to cover my ears, but I had to help hold him down, along with a tech. It took the three of us to keep him on the table.

Every follow-up appointment after that was hard. His blood pressure would spike, and he walked in with visible anxiety.

The timing couldn't have been worse. Alex had been looking forward to tryouts at Furman University for months, but the surgeon made it clear—no activity that might risk shifting the bone. His season was cut short in an instant.

The week was rough for all of us. Alex endured the pain of a complicated break, and at the same time, I was recovering from minor foot surgery. On top of that, Andrew was still dealing with concussion symptoms from the month before. It felt like we were all hobbling along together, each of us carrying our own injury, physical or otherwise.

Our Bond

Through all of it, Alex and I shared a connection that felt unspoken. We both thrived on structure, hated chaos, and leaned toward perfectionism. He understood me, and I understood him. In a household often dominated by Andrew's volatility, Alex was safe and predictable.

And that's what made it so hard when, just as I thought things were finally settling down—Andrew getting the help he needed and Alex shining in school and soccer—Alex began making choices that shook me. Once again, just when I thought I could breathe, the ground shifted beneath my feet.

TWENTY-SIX
METH, MINISTRY, AND MUGSHOTS

Friday Night Lights, Shattered

It was supposed to be a normal high school soccer game—the kind of evening where parents cheered from the bleachers and teenagers played under the glow of stadium lights. Both Andrew and Alex had taken the field. As team captain, Andrew was in his senior year, just weeks away from graduation, the finish line in sight.

Instead, the night unraveled into humiliation.

Josh had pulled his Jeep too close to the fence to avoid paying admission. A sheriff noticed, walked over, and what started as irritation turned into suspicion. The officer smelled drugs. Within minutes, the search began, and the truth spilled out: meth and paraphernalia, sex toys, and a knife.

From the stands, we could see the scene unfold. The deputies handled it quietly, but for Andrew and Alex, the humiliation was seared deep: their father arrested at their game, their classmates whispering, their community watching. His Jeep was towed in plain sight, a final insult. Because Josh had failed to pay alimony and child support, a bench warrant was already waiting. Now he had multiple charges to answer for.

The Boys' Perspective

For Andrew, the timing was cruel. Graduation was weeks away, but instead of walking the halls with joy, he carried the heavy shame of his father's downfall. Whispers followed him. Friends didn't know what to say. Teachers looked at him with pity. Even the boys' soccer coach talked too much, which did nothing to squelch the gossip.

Alex's pain was quieter but no less intense. His silence was its own indictment. He didn't want to talk about it, kept his eyes down, but his fury was unmistakable: furious at the embarrassment, the lies, and that his father couldn't show up clean even for one night that mattered. That pent-up rage would spill out later in ways I could never have predicted.

The game was supposed to be about them, their youth, their future, their milestones. Instead, it became another mugshot for Josh, another scar for my boys. I didn't even recognize the man I had married anymore. His body was gaunt, his face hollow, his teeth rotting from meth.

From Pulpit to Prison

The humiliation cut deeper because of what came before. Just a few years earlier, Josh and I lived a different life: full-time ministry, traveling to share the gospel, and raising our boys in the center of the church and community. We were the family others looked to for faith and stability.

Now, that legacy was gone. Meth had replaced ministry—arrests had replaced altar calls. Instead of a pulpit, Josh's story was written in court records.

Between 2013 and 2020, he was arrested five separate times, generating eight criminal cases in Anderson and Greenville Counties.

Drugs, stolen property, fraud, traffic violations; it read like the rap sheet of a man spiraling out of control. On top of that, he was found in contempt and ordered into Family Court more than a dozen times for failure to pay alimony and child support.

Mercy for the Guilty

As a mother, I was torn in two directions. On one hand, I fought to hold Josh accountable, demanding child support and trying to make him show up for his boys. On the other, I stepped in to shield him from prison, thinking I was sparing Andrew and Alex further humiliation.

In August 2015, while recovering from abdominal surgery, I wrote this letter to the judge:

Letter to the Judge (August 4, 2015)

August 04, 2015

Re: File No. 2013-DR-04-01362

Dear Judge,

My ex-husband, Joshua O, paid me $500 for child support in June, July, and August 2015 for a total of $1,500. I am asking that you credit his child support account and not issue him jail time. I request that he be required to continue paying $500 per month for child support.

I have decided to forgive his alimony debt. Josh and I have agreed that he will pay the child support arrears of $7,067.54 and the current amount due of $1,650. (Please apply his $1,500 credit towards the current amount due.) We have also agreed that he will continue to make monthly child support payments of $500 until the child support arrears are paid in full.

Usually, I am present at these hearings; however, I am recovering from abdominal surgery and am unable to be there today. I may be reached at during the time of the hearing.

Sincerely,

Hailey O.

I didn't do it for him. I did it for my boys. But mercy couldn't rewrite his choices. All I had really done was delay the inevitable.

And then, just eleven days later, I wrote again—this time directly to Judge Herlong:

Letter to Judge Herlong (August 15, 2015)

August 15, 2015

Dear Judge Herlong,

I am writing on behalf of my ex-husband, Joshua O. I am asking that you not send him to prison since our sons, Andrew and Alex, depend each month on his $500 child support payment. We need Josh's payment for food and other necessities. We could not continue to stay in our home without this income.

In addition, it would be detrimental to Andrew and Alex for their father to be unavailable physically and emotionally for an extended period of time. Andrew is 18 years old, and Alex is 16 years old, which is a critical time in their life for which they need their father.

While I agree that Josh has made some poor choices, I believe he has learned his lesson and is not a danger to himself or others. I'm asking that you take into account the negative impact on our sons and choose probation rather than prison time.

Respectfully yours,

Hailey O.

Jeannie's Fall

Josh's second wife, Jeannie, fell with him. Before she met him, she was beautiful, self-sufficient, and working as a surgical tech. After she tied herself to Josh, her world collapsed. She lost her job. She lost custody of her only child when drugs entered the picture. The boys were devastated for Jeannie and her daughter, whom they loved. And soon, the magnificent house fell into foreclosure.

Andrew tried to warn her. Before their marriage in the fall of 2011, he told Jeannie point-blank not to marry his dad. She didn't listen. She was charmed the same way I once was. By the time she realized Josh had repeated the same sins, infidelity and deception now wrapped around meth, it was too late.

The boys stopped visiting. They noticed the paranoia: black curtains nailed over the windows, strangers coming and going at all hours, rooms rented to make extra cash. They suspected what was happening inside those walls. When Jeannie finally admitted Josh had cheated on her, too, it only confirmed what they already knew: history was repeating itself.

The Biggest Blow

The arrest at the soccer game was humiliating, but the deeper blow came later, when Josh was convicted and sentenced to nine months in prison.

For Andrew and Alex, it was both relief and devastation. Relief, because maybe the chaos would stop. Devastation, because it confirmed what they feared: their father wasn't coming back to the life he had once lived.

The contrast was unbearable—from ministry to meth, from sharing the gospel to wearing an ankle monitor, from being their father at home to being another inmate behind bars.

The Shadow They Carried

I told my boys over and over: your father's choices are not your destiny. Still, I could see the shadow it cast. Every arrest, every court date, every broken promise etched itself into their story, even when they didn't want it to.

The night of the soccer game in April 2015 was more than just another arrest. It was the night my sons lost the last shred of hope that their father might change.

From there, the months rolled forward with merciless speed—Andrew's graduation, my surgery, Alex's rise on the soccer field. Despite missing six weeks of school from the assault and another concussion that spring, Andrew graduated with a 3.1 GPA—a quiet miracle carved out of chaos. He even earned the *Outstanding Senior in Automotive Technology* award, proof of the determination that refused to break, even when everything else did.

Each moment fell like a domino against the next. By summer, I was flat on my back in a hospital bed, fighting to recover from major surgery. By fall, Andrew was finding his footing in adulthood, Alex was testing every limit, and Josh was trading the pulpit for a prison sentence.

That year didn't just test me; it pulled at every anchor I had left. Even my job, the one steady ground I had always relied on, was beginning to shift beneath me.

TWENTY-SEVEN
WHEN LIGHTNING STRIKES TWICE

The Perfect Storm

My life felt like a relentless tsunami, wave after crushing wave.

By day, I worked full-time at a psychiatric hospital, coding medical charts while trying to keep food on the table. By night, I wrangled two teenage boys who seemed determined to give me gray hair before I turned forty. Andrew, my oldest, had just graduated with honors, but not before giving me a near heart attack with his high-speed police chase through our neighborhood at 2 a.m. Alex, my youngest, had tested every limit during his sophomore year, even stealing beer from gas stations before finally turning the corner into something better.

And then there was their father. Handcuffed and dragged away from their soccer game in April, his arrest precipitated the start of a legal battle that ended with a two-year prison sentence. I became the only anchor left in their world. While I was still recovering from surgery that summer, I found myself drafting letters to judges on Josh's behalf —not for his sake, but for the boys'—even as his case moved forward.

Meanwhile, my own body was betraying me. Years of complications from breast implants had taken a toll on my immune system, leaving me with chronic abdominal pain, little to no energy, and nights spent staring at the ceiling in stubborn insomnia. By the summer, I was crawling out of a hospital bed after major abdominal surgery, my body still screaming in protest, while at the same time finishing my bachelor's degree and starting my MBA. Apparently, I didn't know how to do anything halfway.

Major Surgery I Couldn't Afford to Take

Since my gallbladder had been removed years earlier, my colon never worked properly. After years of treatments, I finally trusted a surgeon to remove a small section in July 2015. He warned me this was no routine procedure. "More serious than a hysterectomy," he said. "You'll need six weeks off work."

Six weeks! I didn't have six days. I had no PTO left, not after years of doctor's appointments for me, appointments for the boys, and endless court dates with Josh. I agreed to the surgery anyway.

The Color of Regret

The second day after surgery, something went wrong. My pain was so sharp I could barely breathe. The surgeon rushed me back for a follow-up procedure. It worked, but the recovery was brutal. A tube snaked down my nose into my stomach, draining bile into a bucket that hung above my bed—green, the color of sickness.

And every swallow was a reminder of the decision I still hated myself for. Those damn breast implants. I had signed up for beauty and walked away with an immune system in ruins, a body that never worked the same again, and a cascade of surgeries that nearly broke me.

Ten Days Behind Glass

For ten days I lay in that hospital bed. Eight of those days I couldn't eat. My only view was the roof of the building next door, flat, gray, and lifeless. I felt like an inmate staring at concrete walls.

On day seven, desperate for air, Alex snuck me outside in a wheelchair. Even the hospital parking lot felt like heaven.

My Boys, My Lifeline

The bright spot in those days was my boys.

Andrew came every day, steady as a metronome. He had grown into a man seemingly overnight, working full time at O'Reilly Auto Parts, earning his ASE Student Certification, and paying his own bills. His hands were calloused now, but his words had softened. One afternoon he looked me in the eye and said, "I'm sorry for all the grief I caused you, Mom."

This was the same boy who had once fought me at every turn. Now he was dependable, skilled, and proud of his work. He had even placed fifth in the Ford/AAA Auto Skills Competition, earning a $2,000 scholarship. Years earlier, he had been crowned Grand Champion of the BI-LO Invention Convention, already proving he had the creativity and determination to build something from nothing. For the first time, I believed him when he said, "I'll be okay."

Alex came too, every chance he got. His wild streak had cooled, and on the field he was proving himself a leader. His coaches praised him as aggressive, brave, and endlessly coachable, the kind of player any team would want. He had just been named captain of his high school varsity team as a junior, a rare honor. His coach called him "a player who can dribble anyone and still inspire his teammates."

But when he pushed my wheelchair into the sun that July afternoon, he wasn't a star athlete. He was just my boy, giving me back a piece of freedom I thought I had lost.

Walking It Out

On day eight, I was ready to go home, but the surgeon wouldn't release me until I had a bowel movement. For two days, I walked laps around the hospital floor, prune juice in hand, determined to make my body cooperate. Finally, on day ten, it did.

Pale as a ghost and ten pounds lighter, I went home—straight into a sweltering South Carolina summer and the gut punch of a $5,000 bill for an entirely new HVAC unit.

Mercy That Cost Me

But even from that hospital bed, I wasn't just fighting for myself. In August 2015, still raw from surgery, I wrote two letters to judges on Josh's behalf. Not for him, I had long since stopped believing he would change. I wrote them for Andrew and Alex because they needed his child support, and because I thought protecting them meant shielding him.

In one letter, I pleaded that his $500 monthly payment not be cut off. In another, I begged for probation instead of prison, reminding the court that my sons needed their father at such a critical age.

I told myself I was doing the right thing. But as I watched bile drain into that bucket above my bed, I knew the truth: mercy could not rewrite his choices. All I had really done was delay the inevitable.

No Advocate Left

Three weeks later, stitches still raw, I went back to work against the doctor's orders. That same day marked the start of my final semester for my bachelor's degree, just three classes away from graduating magna cum laude. Because I never did things halfway, I also enrolled in two MBA courses with special permission from the provost.

But when I returned to work, my sweet mentor of eighteen months had retired. My new boss looked at me and saw only absences, not the life behind them. She called me into a meeting with the CEO and berated me for my attendance.

She didn't know that I had been an exemplary employee, that I had earned awards, scholarships, and public speaking honors while holding my family together with sheer determination. My former boss had known. She had written me a glowing recommendation letter:

"Hailey is a pleasure to work with and always positive... Her work ethic is impeccable. She is eager to learn and grow... She has a strong work ethic, as demonstrated by continuing her education and working full-time in addition to being a single mom. She is a valued employee."

Alison J. Hale, Director of Quality Management

Reading those words should have lifted me. Instead, I broke down in tears. My body was still healing, and here I was, reduced to a timesheet.

And it wasn't only work that was unraveling. That summer, I had finally ended a painful two-and-a-half-year, on-again, off-again relationship. He had three sons of his own, which only added to the chaos I was already drowning in. At first, I convinced myself we could build a blended family, that maybe love could be enough to knit together all those moving pieces. But cracks appeared quickly.

He wanted me to quit my job. He wanted me to put my degree on hold. He wanted me to stay home and take care of all the boys while he traveled for work.

I had heard that one before.

By then, I was finally starting to see the pattern. I kept attracting narcissists who wanted me small, silent, and dependent. For once, I chose differently. I walked away. It hurt, but it also set me free.

In that moment, I knew I couldn't stay where I was.

What my new boss didn't know was that I had already been submitting applications for a year, clawing my way toward something better. After nineteen rejections, nineteen "we'll be in touch" emails, the largest hospital in South Carolina finally said yes.

It was only a ninety-day contract, not permanent. But it paid nearly double my salary, and it felt like my chance to finally get ahead. For six short weeks, I thought I had caught a break.

But storms don't wait for clear skies. Another one was already forming, and it was about to hit me from behind.

TWENTY-EIGHT

A MOTHER'S EPIC JOURNEY THROUGH DARKNESS

The Sound of Everything Breaking

The rain sounds different when your world is about to end.

It isn't just water tapping the windshield. It's percussion inside my chest, a rhythm I'm trying to match my breath to. December 1, 2015. I-85 southbound at night. That stretch of highway where the lanes feel too narrow, the asphalt disappears beneath your tires, and headlights smear into white and red streaks.

I shouldn't even be here. I should already be at the ceremony—the MBA grant acceptance, proof that all the scraped knees of my life, all the humiliations and near-failures, are finally worth something. My fingers grip the steering wheel, lit by the dashboard glow.

Six weeks into my dream job at the largest hospital in South Carolina. Six weeks of telling myself it's safe to exhale, to believe in good news after nineteen rejections.

The wipers slap the windshield in a chant I can't ignore: you're-gonna-make-it, you're-gonna-make-it, you're-gonna-make-it.

Up ahead, brake lights flare—a sudden constellation of red scattered across the blacktop. My stomach tightens. This is the stretch where dreams stall out in mangled wreckage, where one bad decision redraws the entire story of your life.

I tap the brake. Then press harder. The car slows. Stops.

For a single, precious heartbeat, relief floods me.

Warmth spreads through my chest as I picture the evening still waiting: handshakes, applause, the affirmation that after years of clawing forward, I'm finally stepping into the light. Tomorrow, I'll tell my boys. Maybe they'll see their mom not as someone endlessly scrambling to survive but as someone winning, someone worth admiring.

Headlights fill my rearview mirror—too fast, too close, too late.

I turn to my left to see who's closing in, a quick reflex I'll later regret.

My stomach plummets. Not now. Not when things are finally starting to come together—when the years of struggle, single motherhood, and scraping by are beginning to feel like they meant something.

Time fractures.

The jolt snaps me against the headrest, a solid thud that vibrates down my spine. Not catastrophic, not cinematic. Just enough to make me pause, to take stock, to thank God for padded seats and modern engineering. The world shudders, then goes still.

I sit frozen, engine humming in the hush after impact. My breath is shallow, measured. I expect the worst when I climb out, twisted metal, shattered taillights, visible proof of the collision I felt. Instead: barely a dent. The car wears its damage lightly, like a secret.

That's the part no one tells you: sometimes the blows that devastate don't leave marks you can point to. Sometimes what shatters isn't the body or the machine, but the rhythm of your life —the fragile belief that you were finally safe.

I turn my head. Or try to. My neck balks, stiff and resistant, a warning I ignore. Probably just whiplash. Nothing that will still matter by morning. Nothing serious.

Blue lights strobe the wet highway. Firefighters, police officers, strangers moving in and out of my vision like actors in someone else's play. Their voices sound muffled, filtered through cotton. Do you need to go to the hospital? No. I just want to go home. It's been a long day, my first class at the new job, the ceremony I've now missed, and all the small victories that suddenly feel very far away.

What I don't yet understand is this: some accidents break more than metal and glass. Some accidents slice time itself into "before" and "after." And once that cut is made, you spend years trying to stitch the pieces together again.

I close my eyes and strain to remember what was on my mind a second before the impact. The applause. The promise of momentum. The fragile hope of things finally going right.

But all I hear now is the rain, endless and insistent, and the faint whisper of a life already slipping from me, though I don't yet know it.

The woman who walks away from this wreckage won't be the same woman who drove into it.

Not that night. Not ever again.

The Descent into Darkness

"No whiplash. Just a mild concussion." That's what the ER doctor said, cheerful and brisk as if her words could erase what my body already knew. "Take two days off, rest up. You'll be fine by Monday."

Simple. Reassuring. A promise that became a lie.

Because the pain didn't fade. It grew. Migraines like lightning strikes detonated behind my left eye, each one strong enough to make me vomit, to make me crawl into a darkened room and beg for silence.

Ten days later came the graduation I had waited a lifetime for. This was supposed to be the moment—the culmination of the dream that had begun when I was a teen mom and never finished high school properly, scraping by with just the two dual-enrollment classes I needed for a diploma. Years as a stay-at-home mom had followed, a decision I never regretted but one that had delayed every plan.

Now, at last, it was here. Graduation day. The moment I had inched my way toward for nearly two decades. But the crash had left me with more than lingering headaches. The concussion meant I couldn't tolerate light, noise, or long stretches on the road. Even the motion of the windshield wipers sent searing shocks through my skull. Driving was out of the question.

So Andrew and Alex drove the four hours to Myrtle Beach for the ceremony, steady and protective in a way that reminded me just how much they had grown. My parents flew in to celebrate. Coastal Carolina University, my school, had even published a feature about my journey.

Graduate Hailey O. Takes Unusual Path to Degree

By Mona Prufer

Hailey O. is not your traditional four-year college-degree-seeking student. It has taken her 19 years to earn a bachelor's degree, but she's raised a family along the way, gathered various accolades, two more degrees (one she's still working on) and will graduate magna cum laude at Coastal Carolina University's winter commencement ceremony on Dec. 11.

That's how journalist Mona Prufer began the article Coastal Carolina published about my story. It felt like the ribbon on everything I had fought for. (See *the full article after this chapter.*)

It should have been a day full of light. But instead of basking in the moment, I sat under that cavernous ceiling with my skull pounding, sunglasses on indoors, every clink of silverware at the celebratory lunch stabbing through my head. My dad had just had eye surgery, so in the photos we're both wearing sunglasses. It looks like a joke. It wasn't. Everything was too bright, too loud, too much.

Days stretched into weeks. Weeks into months. And when I couldn't go back to work—when my body refused the dream job I had fought so hard for—it slipped through my fingers like it had never belonged to me at all.

I remember looking up at my ceiling, whispering to God through gritted teeth: *Really? After everything? After all the fights I've survived, this is what You hand me now?*

The diagnosis came later: traumatic brain injury (TBI). Three words that carried a weight I couldn't hold. Soldiers, athletes, people who had earned their scars in ways the world understood—that's who had TBIs. Not me. So what did that make me?

A recluse, for starters.

I darkened my windows. I padded through my own home in sunglasses and earplugs like a fugitive from sound and light. I couldn't tolerate screens—no computer, no TV, no late-night scrolling to distract me from my pain. Books blurred. Music stabbed. Even driving had to be rationed to thirty minutes before agony forced me to pull over. The simple rhythm of windshield wipers sent searing shocks down the left side of my head, leaving me dizzy and nauseous.

If I ignored the symptoms and pushed through, there would be hell to pay for days, when I couldn't get out of bed from the extreme pain triggered by what most people would consider normal activities.

Most days, the bedroom became my cage. Just me, four walls, and a ceiling I memorized in every crack and shadow. My once relentless pace—classes, work, soccer games, ambition—collapsed into silence.

And in that silence came the storm: anger, grief, disbelief, and the gnawing fear of what my boys' lives would look like if their mother never recovered.

From the boys' perspective, it was torture. They had already endured the shame of their father's public arrest. Now they had to watch their mother suffer behind drawn curtains. They hated seeing me weak. They didn't say it, but their eyes did. They hovered, trying to help, but I saw the helplessness in their faces—the dread of losing me, too.

I didn't yet know it, but I was stepping into a different kind of darkness. Not the kind you drive through on I-85. The kind that lives inside your psyche, steals your momentum, and whispers that maybe you'll never get your life back.

Not Your Traditional Student

Graduate Hailey O. takes unusual path to degree

by Prufer

Hailey O. is not your traditional, four-year college-degree seeking student. It has taken her 19 years to earn a bachelor's degree, but she's raised a family along the way, gathered various accolades, two more degrees (one she's still working on) and should graduate magna cum laude at Coastal Carolina University's winter commencement ceremony on Dec. 11.

She is one of 583 candidates eligible to march in the ceremony. As a distance-learning student, she has been on CCU's campus only four times; this December graduation will be her fifth visit, and it's one she wouldn't miss for the world.

The Florida native started out with an ambitious plan to finish high school a year early to get a jumpstart on college and her career goals. But an unplanned pregnancy derailed those plans for 14 years as she concentrated on her growing family.

Two children later, O's marriage ended, and she realized she was in a desperate situation. "The most humbling experience of all was when I had to apply for Medicaid and food stamps," she recalls. She knew that more education was her answer out of a downward spiral. She enrolled in a nearby technical college and completed an associate degree in health information management.

"As soon as I graduated, I wanted to continue my education with a bachelor's degree, and found that Coastal offered an online health administration degree program," she says. "The reason I chose health administration was because I believed that I could make a difference in the evolving health care industry, while at the same time improve patient care.

"I chose CCU because after researching its program, I was confident it would prepare me for influential leadership positions within the health care field."

O says her experience at CCU has been marked by "strong connection to faculty members" such as lecturer Kristi Forbus, her academic adviser, who have supported and encouraged her, as have the Writing Center, the Office and Financial Aid, and the Women in Philanthropy and Leadership (WIPL) organization, which awarded her as the first recipient of the organization's endowed scholarship.

Along the way, while working full time and raising her sons, O racked up plenty of accomplishments. In addition to the WIPL scholarship, she was inducted into Omicron Delta Kappa because of her 3.9 GPA, she was nominated for the University Distinguished Student Award, she received the award for Outstanding Student Achievement in Health Administration, "Who's Who Among Students in American Universities and Colleges," and she became a public speaker for WIPL (at an earlier conference) and for the Office of Philanthropy.

"There is something very special about Coastal's unique dynamic, and I will be forever grateful for my positive experience here," says O.

"When I gave my speech at the Donor's Recognition Reception, I shared how I wanted to get my MBA at CCU. However, since there was not a fully online program, I had planned to get my MBA at North Greenville University. After my speech, Provost Ralph Byington approached me and said he would do what it took to keep me at CCU as an online MBA student."

In addition to finishing three final undergraduate courses, O will also receive her MBA in December 2016, which was made possible through collaboration with Byington, Business Dean Barbara Ritter and Robert Reed, student services program coordinator in the E. Craig Wall Sr. College of Business Administration.

Recently, she was granted a graduate assistantship through the business college and will be assisting faculty members Ken Small, Frances Richmond and Ellen Hayward. The stipend will cover graduate tuition for the semester, which means if she keeps the assistantship for one more semester, then all of her three degrees will have been 100 percent financed through grants, scholarships and the assistantship.

"I feel like I've won the lottery!" says O.

She graduated with an associate degree in health information management and became a registered health information technician in 2013. In December 2016, she hopes to become CCU's first online MBA graduate. If she succeeds in that endeavor, she will have earned three degrees in four years.

In case you think O is resting on the laurels of her upcoming graduation, think again. She has pinpointed her long-term career goal, which is to specialize in operations and become COO of a large health care organization. She has already taken a big step in that direction.

After two years of submitting 19 applications to Greenville Heath System, the largest health care organization in the region, she was hired as a consultant to teach the new electronic medical records software to employees. She is also working on establishing a Greenville chapter of the American Business Women's Association (ABWA) since there is not one in Greenville.

O's sons are on their way to achieving their own goals also: Eighteen-year-old Andrew graduated high school last year and is taking a year off to decide on a major. He works full time at an auto parts store.

Alex is 16, loves his biomed course at Wren High School and wants to be a physician. He volunteered at a hospital this past summer, is involved with a junior leadership program at the local Chamber of Commerce and plans to apply to CCU's Honors College in a few months. Both boys will be in the audience come Dec. 11 with their grandparents Ray and Betty Violin, from Yuma, Ariz., to watch their mom pick up her long-anticipated degree.

"I want everyone to know how blessed I have been by CCU's generosity," says this focused, high-achieving woman. "I am truly appreciative for the opportunities that I have been given and am a Chanticleer for LIFE! My life has been completely transformed as a result of my positive experience at CCU, and I will be forever grateful!"

TWENTY-NINE

HOPE, ETCHED IN SKIN

The Medical Maze

Doctors' offices blur together after a while, the beige walls, the smell of antiseptic, the rustle of paper gowns. Each one different, but all of them the same: long waits, cold stethoscopes, and practiced sympathy that doesn't always reach the eyes.

I cycled through them like stations on a dial. Family physicians, neurologists, and specialists at MUSC. I tried massage, chiropractic care, acupuncture, and physical therapy, anything that seemed promising. Medical providers ordered scans, tests, and bloodwork. They tilted my head this way, tapped reflexes, scribbled notes.

I was even desperate enough to try Botox injected across my scalp to calm the headaches—the medical kind insurance paid for, not the vanity injections I had only ever known about as a luxury I couldn't afford.

Every appointment ended with some version of the same sentence: "Traumatic brain injuries take time. Give it a year. Then you'll know what the rest of your life will look like."

A year? To learn that the life I'd clawed back could be gone forever? No. That didn't work for me.

The medical system wanted me to settle into the waiting room of my own life. But I had already learned, the hard way, that if you don't fight for yourself, no one else will.

Some nights, lying in the dark with my skull splitting, I thought about giving up. But every time, something inside whispered: *Not yet. God isn't finished.*

Too many times to count, my sons took me to the ER for another migraine that wouldn't cease for days. Nothing helped. No drug, not even narcotics or opioids, offered relief. The only thing that dulled it was a nerve stabilizer called Neurontin.

When the pain got so out of control—days on end with no relief—the only option was for one of my sons to drive me to the ER for a shot to dull the pain. It never went away completely, but if I could get the vomiting, nausea, and room-spinning to simply dull, I could live with that.

And then one night, prayer and desperation braided together into a wild idea. I typed it into the search bar with hesitant fingers: surgery after concussion.

What popped up wasn't what my doctors had told me to expect. It was a name—Dr. Ivica Ducic, Washington D.C.—and a string of stories about college athletes whose concussions had turned into years of agony. Their symptoms mirrored mine: migraines that wouldn't quit, light and noise that sliced like knives. And yet... they'd found relief.

Nerve damage. That was the missing word. Not one of my doctors had mentioned it. But here it was, the possibility that my pain wasn't just random, wasn't just "time." That it had a cause—and maybe even a solution.

The Miracle Check

Within weeks, I was on a plane. My head throbbed with every pressurized shift in altitude, but I clutched hope like a boarding pass. When I sat in Dr. Ducic's office, he didn't dismiss me. He listened. He examined. And then he said the words I'd been waiting for: "Your occipital nerve is entrapped by blood vessels. Surgery can help."

It wasn't a guarantee. But it was the first real answer I'd had in months.

There was just one problem.

The deductible. $3,750.

Money I didn't have. Money that might as well have been a million for a single mom who hadn't been able to work for almost an entire year.

I left his office with equal parts hope and dread, clutching a folder of paperwork and praying all the way back to the airport. "God, if this is really the path You've laid out for me, I need You to show me. I need You to make a way."

The day I came home from D.C., my mailbox held an envelope I almost ignored. No return address I recognized. Thin, ordinary, the kind of thing you toss onto the counter without opening.

But something told me to tear it open right there in the driveway.

A check.

$3,795.

I had to blink twice, run my finger over the numbers, to make sure I wasn't hallucinating. Three years earlier, someone had owed me money. So long ago I'd forgotten. My ex-husband had filed his taxes expecting a refund, but the state had intercepted it and rerouted it... to me.

On the exact day I needed it.

For almost the exact amount of my deductible.

I stood in the driveway with the check in my hands, staring in disbelief as rain dripped down my coat, and let out a laugh that sounded suspiciously like a sob.

People can call it karma, coincidence, or divine intervention. But I knew. God had known before I did what I would need, and when. He had timed it down to the day, a reminder that even in the wilderness, He hadn't forgotten me.

I pressed the paper to my chest and whispered, "Thank You." For the first time in a year, hope didn't just flicker. It burned.

First Surgery – January 2017

The hospital in D.C. smelled of antiseptic and quiet dread. The kind of silence that hangs in pre-op rooms, broken only by the hiss of oxygen and the shuffle of nurses' shoes.

I lay on the narrow bed with a flimsy gown tied at the back, staring at the ceiling tiles that all looked the same but somehow felt like they were watching me. A nurse clipped monitors to my chest, each beep pulling me closer to the moment I couldn't avoid.

Dr. Ducic appeared at my side, calm and steady, even comforting, as if he were about to fix a leaking faucet instead of open my head. He explained again how he'd locate the blood vessels strangling my occipital nerve, how he'd move them aside, how maybe—the fire in my skull would finally go out.

I nodded, pretending courage. Inside, I was bargaining with God. Please. Please let this be the answer. Please let me go home to my boys with more than pain to offer them.

When I woke, my scalp felt heavy, the skin tight and throbbing. The incision was larger than I'd pictured, but tucked into my hairline. I found myself praying I'd never have to face cancer and the kind of baldness that would bare every scar. Bandages itched, pain meds dulled the edges. But underneath the haze, even just one day later, something felt different.

The headaches weren't gone, but muted. Less constant. For the first time in over a year, I felt the faintest stirring of relief.

Hope bloomed—reckless, fragile, but alive. Maybe this is the end of my nightmare.

When Hope Collapsed

That hope didn't last. By summer, I tried to step back into my old rhythm, re-enrolling in MBA courses and picking up pieces of the life I had abandoned. But within weeks, the migraines roared back. Debilitating, merciless, as if mocking me for believing I had outrun them.

Withdrawing from classes broke something in me. The disappointment was deeper than academics, it was soul-deep. I had dared to dream, and the dream had collapsed again.

Which is why, when I heard about stem cell therapy in Park City, Utah, I was ready to gamble everything.

Stem Cell Replacement – July 2017

The clinic smelled less like a hospital and more like hope dressed up in science. Sleek furniture, glossy pamphlets, posters of smiling patients who had found healing here.

I wanted to be one of them.

The doctor spoke with the kind of confidence that hooks desperate people like me: stem cells could regenerate damaged nerves, restore function, rebuild what pain had destroyed.

It wasn't covered by insurance. It would drain what little savings I had left, push my credit cards deeper into the red. But I signed the papers anyway. What was the price of freedom from pain?

I remember the moments leading up to it more than the procedure itself. I was asleep while it happened, but the familiar, chemical bite of anesthesia filled my lungs and anchored itself in memory. They pierced my hip to extract the stem cells, then injected them into my scalp. A deep ache spread through my head as I imagined the cells like tiny soldiers, marching into battle, rebuilding me from the inside out.

But weeks passed. Then months.

Nothing changed.

The headaches stayed, merciless. Worse, scar tissue formed at the injection sites, adding new layers of pain to the old ones. My bank account was empty. My body was angrier than ever. And my hope, that last thin thread, snapped.

I sank into depression so heavy it felt like drowning in wet cement. For the first time, I didn't see a way forward. I, the woman who always found another door to kick open, finally stood in front of a wall too high to climb.

By then, I was surviving on scraps. In the blur of pain and bills, I crossed a line I once swore I never would. At the time, I told myself it was temporary, just another way to keep us afloat. But deep down, I knew it was changing me. I didn't have the words for it yet, but I was stepping into a survival mode that mirrored Josh's chaos in ways that haunted me later.

Losing Dignity, Gaining Survival

No longer able to outwork or outthink my circumstances, I crossed a line I thought I never would. I stepped into the oldest profession in history. I am not proud of it. It's a part of my story that still carries shame. But survival demanded it. Some nights I was paid $500, sometimes $1,000. That money meant the lights stayed on, the mortgage was covered, and there was food on the table. It was survival, pure and raw.

But the trade came with a cost no paycheck could cover. Every dollar carried the weight of my values, my faith, the mother I wanted to be. I thought about Josh and the ways he had betrayed those same Christian values, and the bitter irony that my choices now mirrored his compromises in a twisted way.

One evening, after I splurged on a restaurant we usually couldn't afford, one of my boys looked across the table and said, "Wow, Mom. I don't know what you're doing, but I hope you keep doing it. We really appreciate this."

I smiled. But inside, I broke. I wanted them to see me as strong, steady, unshakable. Instead, I carried the secret of how far I had fallen, praying they would never know the truth.

A Means to an End

I had fought so hard to keep us afloat—hustling handbags, flipping thrift store finds, even working briefly as an escort. But no matter how creative or desperate my survival became, one truth never changed: I couldn't escape the pain in my head.

It was always there, relentless, mocking me. The migraines shaped every decision, limited every option, and kept me tethered to a body that refused to cooperate.

Each procedure left its mark, physical and emotional, until I barely recognized the woman I had once been. My body was carved by surgeries, my spirit weighed down by survival, and still the migraines refused to release me. It felt like every option had been tried, every avenue exhausted, every hope crushed. I had carried the weight of illness, betrayal, and shame for so long that I wondered if this was all my life would ever be.

By October 2017, I had had enough of half-measures and was done with miracle cures and false hope. If I were going to live again, I had to take the most drastic step yet: surgery to remove the damaged nerves entirely.

If there were one final chance to reclaim my life, I would take it. Even if it meant one more scar. Even if it meant the risk of making the pain worse. It was the last cut I would ever agree to, and it would either give me back my life or take the last pieces of it with it.

THIRTY

THE FINAL CUT

Scars and Surrender

October 2017—I lay on a surgical bed with a line of stitches waiting to mark the back of my scalp.

This was not my first surgery, not even my second. It was the last chance I had left—the decision to cut out the damaged nerves that had stolen two years of my life.

Even if this surgery failed, I had decided: the pain, the betrayal, and the years of survival would no longer define me.

I would learn to reframe the pain—to see in it the beginnings of strength, resilience, even unexpected silver linings.

The room hummed with machines, sterile and cold, while fear curled through my veins like fire.

Best case: the migraines would vanish, and I would reclaim my life.

Worst case: the pain would only deepen.

I closed my eyes and whispered the prayer I had prayed too many times to count:

God, either heal me or help me carry this.

When I woke, the pain was raw, electric, my hairline crisscrossed with stitches. I looked in the mirror and joked to the boys that I resembled Frankenstein, but the truth was I felt scarred in more ways than one.

And yet—something shifted.

Within weeks, the constant, crushing headaches began to ease. For the first time in two years, I could lace up my sneakers, step onto a treadmill, and move without my head punishing me. It felt like being released from prison.

By January 2018, I could finally say the words I hadn't dared to believe:

"I am pain-free."

That freedom gave me something I hadn't had in years—momentum.

I returned to my studies with a renewed determination that felt fierce, intent on finishing what migraines had stolen. I stepped back into my career, no longer surviving by scraps and side hustles, but building toward stability.

And while I was rebuilding, so were my boys.

Andrew was thriving as a personal trainer at the YMCA, studying for his CrossFit certification while pursuing a degree in kinesiology. The same discipline that once helped him rebuild after multiple concussions now fueled his desire to help others heal their own bodies. His natural warmth and steady work ethic made him a favorite among clients and colleagues alike, a quiet leader who inspired by example.

Alex, meanwhile, graduated from high school in 2017 with honors and earned a partial athletic scholarship to Southern Wesleyan University, where he quickly became a starting player as a freshman. That fall, he scored an unforgettable forty-yard goal that tied the NCCAA Regional Championship and sent his team into double overtime, helping secure their victory and a trip to nationals.

Off the field, he showed the same determination, managing twenty-six baristas as the Human Resources Manager at the campus coffee shop. His maturity, leadership, and resilience—especially after a devastating knee injury that sidelined him for a season—became the foundation of his growth both as an athlete and as a man.

For years, my life had been nothing but reaction—patching holes, hustling for survival, clinging to scraps of hope while trying to keep my boys afloat. But this moment marked a shift.

I could not change the past, but I could choose how I carried it.

When Perseverance Isn't Enough

Perseverance had carried me through a lifetime of storms—teen motherhood, betrayal, bankruptcy, illness, and now a brain injury that nearly silenced me for good.

I had learned how to push through when everything in me wanted to quit.

But here's what I discovered in the stillness after the surgery:

Perseverance alone wasn't enough.

Perseverance can keep you breathing, but it can't give you vision.

It can get you through the night, but it can't tell you how to live when morning comes.

What I needed wasn't just endurance.

I needed a **rewrite.**

That's when I realized: every scar, every setback, every desperate prayer had been pointing to something bigger than survival. They were pointing to a framework that could help anyone take the story that tried to break them and turn it into leverage for lasting change.

That became **The Rewrite Framework™.**

You Are the Author of Your Story

Doctors, bosses, spouses—even well-meaning friends—tried to write my ending for me.

If I had believed them, my story would have ended in defeat.

Never hand the pen of your life story to someone else.

Even if your hand shakes—or bleeds—keep writing.

Your hardest seasons can become the beginning of your strength.

What feels like unraveling is often the start of rebuilding.

Pain—no matter how deep—isn't the end of your story.

It can be the very place where your deeper strength begins to take root.

Rewrite the Story That Tried to Break You

The hardest part of my healing wasn't the accident, the surgeries, or even the years of darkness in my bedroom.

It was facing the truth that the story I thought would end me was actually the one meant to teach me how to live differently.

We don't get to choose our collisions—the headlights in the rearview, the diagnosis, the betrayal that knocks the wind out of us.

But we do get to choose what comes next.

We get to decide whether the pain becomes a prison or a portal.

For me, the turning point wasn't when the migraines stopped.

It was when I realized that every setback, every *no*, every scar was preparing me to carry something bigger than myself—a framework to help others walk through their own breaking and come out stronger.

That's what I call **Strategies That Stick®**—truths that anchor you when life tries to rip the ground out from under you.

They're not theories. They're field-tested—born from nights I cried into a pillow, days I couldn't open the blinds, and flights across the country chasing doctors who might hold an answer.

Author Reflection: Stepping Into the Rewrite

If you're reading this, maybe you've been holding your own kind of pain—the invisible kind that doesn't show up on scans but still shapes every part of your life. Maybe you've tried to outrun it, fix it, pray it away, or just survive it. I understand that ache. I lived there for years.

But what I learned on the other side of the operating table is this: the goal isn't to go back to who you were before the pain. The goal is to become someone new because of it.

The scars, the detours, the disappointments—they aren't wasted. They are invitations to start again, differently this time. To reframe your pain, embrace your reality, and work through the obstacles that tried to break you.

So if you're ready, take my hand. Together, we'll begin the process that changed everything for me—**The Rewrite Framework™**—and learn how to turn the story that once hurt you into the story that now heals you.

If you're ready, let's begin where all rewrites do—with a new lens.

Let's learn how to *Reframe Your Pain.*

Want the exact reflection questions and frameworks that helped me turn trauma into transformation?

Scan this QR code to download the full R.E.W.R.I.T.E. Framework™ + EPIC System — the same tools I used to turn rock bottom into rocket fuel... and guide others through theirs.

Inside, you'll get:

☑ **Guided Reflection Questions** for every chapter in Parts I & II

☑ A one-page **R.E.W.R.I.T.E.™ Cheat Sheet** to reclaim your power

☑ The full **EPIC Framework** to turn healing into impact

These aren't just "nice to have" tools —

They're a **map back to yourself... and forward into purpose.**

Scan me!

Scan to Start Your Rewrite

(Instant download. No spam. Just soul-level strategies that work.)

➡ Or visit: **epicimpact.com**

PART 2

PART II THE R.E.W.R.I.T.E. FRAMEWORK

THE SEVEN STEPS TO HELP YOU REFRAME WHAT BROKE YOU—SO YOU CAN RISE IN STRENGTH, LEAD WITH PURPOSE, AND WALK IN FREEDOM.

THIRTY-ONE
REFRAME YOUR PAIN

Find Meaning in the Breaking

For a long time, I believed pain was punishment—proof I had failed somewhere. But I have learned something far more powerful: pain is preparation.

Some pain does not announce itself—it simply shows up. A diagnosis. A betrayal. A dream that shatters the moment you thought you were finally steady. It leaves you breathless, questioning everything, reaching for the reason why.

You see, pain does not come to destroy you; it comes to reveal you.

The freedom you are searching for is not waiting on new circumstances; it is waiting on a new perspective.

Here is the truth: ***being a victim and choosing a victim mentality are not the same thing.***

> Being a victim is something that happened to you. But a victim mentality begins when you remain stuck in "Why me?" instead of stepping forward into "What is next?"
>
> You can honor your hurt without building a home in it.

When my life unraveled through loss and heartbreak, I thought the pain would bury me. But it became something far different.

Loss, betrayal, and illness stripped everything I thought I could depend on. Yet each breaking became a birthplace—soil where new strength began to grow and God started rewriting my story.

The Turning Point

Viktor Frankl wrote in *Man's Search for Meaning,* "When we are no longer able to change a situation, we are challenged to change ourselves." That single truth reframed everything for me.

For years, I tried to fix what was broken—relationships, businesses, even my sense of worth. The turning point came when I realized that transformation does not begin when circumstances change; it begins when perspective does.

Frankl's words taught me that meaning can coexist with suffering. The question is not "Why is this happening?" It is "What is this teaching me?" When you shift from control to curiosity, pain becomes a teacher rather than a tormentor.

The Mindset Shift

Pain invites you to one of two places: bitterness or becoming. You can choose resentment, or you can choose revelation.

When I finally stopped fighting my pain and started listening to it, I began to notice patterns. Every ending that looked like a burial was actually planting ground for something new.

When our business failed, I thought I had lost my calling. Instead, it led me to purpose-driven storytelling. When migraines stole my health, I thought I had lost my strength. Instead, I learned that rest could be holy.

That truth does not erase the ache, but it gives it purpose.

You may not see it now, but the pain that feels unbearable today could be the soil where your future strength grows. The breaking is not proof you are weak; it is proof you are being rebuilt.

Faith in the Fire

There were nights when I prayed for rescue and received silence. When I begged for clarity and found only confusion. But faith reminded me that God's silence is not His absence. He was working beneath the surface—not removing my pain, but redeeming it.

When I look back, I see His fingerprints all over the very places I thought He had abandoned. Every closed door became a redirection. Every disappointment became an anchor for deeper trust.

Faith taught me that surrender is not giving up. It is letting go of the illusion of control and trusting the process of growth.

Living the Reframe

Reframing pain is not about pretending it does not hurt. It is about looking at it through the lens of purpose.

It is asking, "How is this shaping me?" instead of "Why me?"

The moment you begin to reframe, your story shifts. The obstacle becomes an opportunity. The loss becomes a lesson. The wound becomes wisdom.

This is not toxic positivity. It is spiritual resilience. It is refusing to let pain define you while allowing it to refine you.

Your Rewrite Begins Here

Maybe you are standing in the ruins of something you loved—a relationship, a dream, a version of yourself. Maybe you have been asking God to end the storm when He is inviting you to find Him in it.

You do not have to understand your pain to be transformed by it. You only have to stop running from it.

Reframing does not erase the past; it reclaims it. It reminds you that even what tried to break you can become what builds you.

So today, choose to believe that this moment, however painful, is not a punishment. It is preparation.

Reflection Prompts

- What pain in your story might actually be preparing you for something greater?
- How could you shift from asking "Why me?" to "What now?"
- What meaning might you find in the part of your story that still hurts?

THIRTY-TWO
EMBRACE REALITY

Courage to Stand Where You Are

There comes a moment when denial stops protecting you and starts preventing you.

For me, that moment came in the silence when everything fell apart. I had spent years managing the mess and calling it faith, convincing myself that if I just prayed harder, it would all make sense.

But no amount of pretending could fix what I refused to face.

One morning, I caught my reflection and didn't recognize the woman staring back. She looked strong, but I knew she was running on fumes. That was the day I whispered the truth I'd been avoiding: *I'm not okay.*

Naming the truth didn't break me—it built a bridge back to myself.

The Turning Point

Beth Moore captures it beautifully in her book *Chasing Vines: Finding Your Way to an Immensely Fruitful Life*:

"You may think you've been buried, but you've actually been planted."

That truth became my lifeline.

What I thought was the end—a marriage crumbling, dreams dissolving—was actually the beginning of something new. I had mistaken God's planting for punishment. But the dark soil wasn't the grave; it was the ground where roots were forming.

The moment I stopped trying to fix the past and started asking what could grow from it, everything shifted. Honesty didn't destroy me. It rebuilt me.

The Cost of Pretending

Pretending is heavy. It keeps you stuck between who you were and who you're becoming.

I had built a life that looked fine on the outside but felt hollow within. I smiled through heartbreak, worked through exhaustion, and prayed through fear, hoping no one would see the cracks.

The more I performed, the more disconnected I felt—from my purpose, my peace, and my faith.

Naming the truth was terrifying. It meant acknowledging the marriage that had failed, the dreams that had died, and the exhaustion that prayer alone couldn't fix. Yet the moment I stopped defending the illusion, I made room for healing to begin.

Peace begins where pretending ends.

Radical Acceptance

Acceptance doesn't mean agreement. It means choosing reality over resistance.

After my marriage ended, I replayed conversations endlessly, looking for a version where it all worked out. But replaying pain doesn't rewrite it—it just keeps you stuck in the scene.

So I made a new commitment: to see my life as it was, not as I wished it were. I began writing small truths in my journal:

This is my life right now.

God can still do something with it.

I don't have to understand to trust.

Each statement became an act of surrender—not to defeat, but to growth. Radical acceptance didn't make my situation easier, but it made my heart lighter. It turned my prayers from "God, change this" to "God, change me in this."

When You Refuse to Settle

Embracing reality is only half the work. The rest is refusing to settle there.

When you name what's true, you take back your power to choose what happens next.I stopped asking God to change the story and started asking Him to change me in it. I stopped trying to fix other people and started focusing on becoming whole myself.

That's when quiet progress began to appear—new friendships, unexpected opportunities, and a slow rebuilding of confidence. Life didn't magically improve, but I did.

You don't have to accept less than what God intended just because you've been hurt. Embracing truth means saying, *This happened*, while refusing to let it define who you are.

The Freedom of Honesty

Looking back, I see that truth was never my enemy. It was my invitation.

Honesty stripped away everything false until only what was real remained. I realized I didn't need to have all the answers; I just needed the courage to stop hiding from them.

Honesty didn't end my story; it gave peace permission to enter.

When I stopped pretending everything was fine, peace finally had room to grow. And that peace didn't come from fixing the past. It came from standing firmly in the present and trusting that God could still write something beautiful from the broken pieces.

Reflection Prompts

- What truth have you been avoiding because it feels too painful to face?
- How could naming that truth bring more peace than pretending?
- Where might God be inviting you to start again, right where you are?

THIRTY-THREE

WORK THROUGH OBSTACLES

Choose Renewal Over Captivity

Every transformation begins with a mental shift.

A **captive mindset** clings to control, denies pain, and resists change.

A **freedom mindset** faces truth head-on, releases the illusion of control, and believes that renewal can rise even from ruins.

Freedom doesn't remove obstacles—it **reshapes how you meet them.**

You can't pray your way out of every storm, but you can **choose how you walk through them.**

There comes a moment when denial stops protecting you and starts preventing you.

For me, that moment came in the silence after everything collapsed— the betrayal, the financial wreckage, the exhaustion of pretending I was fine. I had spent years holding my world together by sheer willpower, but inside, I was breaking.

One morning, I opened my journal and wrote the words I'd been avoiding: "I am not okay." I looked strong to everyone else, but I knew I was running on empty.

Honesty didn't weaken me; it released me.

The Power of Honesty

Authors Dan and Chip Heath wrote in *Switch: How to Change Things When Change Is Hard*, "*What looks like resistance is often a lack of clarity.*"

Those words changed how I viewed my obstacles. For years, I believed I was resisting change, but I was not resisting at all—I was unclear about what needed to change. I wanted transformation without truth, healing without honesty, and movement without clarity.

But clarity only comes when we stop hiding from what is real.

I prayed for God to mend what broke, yet fear kept me from admitting how deep the fractures ran. When I finally named the truth—first before God, then within myself—something shifted. Honesty never ends your story; it rebuilds it from the inside out.

Facing Obstacles with Honesty

Embracing reality signals courage, not approval. It means choosing truth over illusion when denial feels safer.

Obstacles reveal the corners of life we cannot command—loss, disappointment, betrayal, fear—yet our vision shapes whether we walk free or remain captive.

When my marriage collapsed, I replayed every conversation, chasing a version where everything healed. But replaying pain tightens the chains that memory forged. The past holds power only until we stop feeding it.

So I began writing simple truths in my journal:

This is my life right now. *It will not always look like this.*

God can still do something with it. *I will believe even when I cannot see.*

I do not have to understand the big picture to trust. *My part is simply to take the next step.*

Each sentence was a small act of courage. Not a declaration of defeat, but of determination.

Radical honesty became my turning point. Once I stopped pretending, I could finally see the next step forward.

Obstacles and Perspective

Obstacles are not permanent walls. They are circumstances we cannot change. However, when we shift our perspective, those same circumstances lose their power. The situation may remain the same, but our vision transforms—and that change alone can reshape our entire world.

Here is what that shift looks like in real life:

Obstacle	Captive Mindset	Freedom Mindset
A relationship ends	"I will never be loved again."	"That chapter closed, but I am still worthy of love."
Job loss or career setback	"I failed. I am stuck."	"This is difficult, but it may be clearing space for what is next."
Betrayal or deep hurt	"I can never trust anyone again."	"That wound hurts, but I can still choose healthy relationships."
Delayed dreams or failed plans	"Nothing ever works out for me."	"This may not be failure. It may be redirection."
Fear of the unknown	"I must control everything to be safe."	"I can walk in faith even when I do not see the full path."

Freedom does not mean pretending the obstacle is gone. It means refusing to let it define your identity or dictate your future.

A victim can still find peace and freedom even in pain.

But choosing a victim mentality creates captivity, where resentment and fear hold you hostage. The difference is not in what happens to you, but in how you choose to see it.

From Resistance to Renewal

Truth does not always feel like relief at first. It can feel like loss. But every time I chose honesty over illusion, peace followed.

I stopped asking, "Why me?" and started asking, "What's next?" I stopped trying to fix people and began focusing on becoming whole myself.

That is when something unexpected happened. My strength returned. New opportunities surfaced. Friendships deepened. Nothing about my situation changed overnight, but everything inside me did.

Resistance faded because clarity replaced confusion.

Refusing to Settle

Embracing reality is not the same as settling for it. Once you see clearly, you gain the power to choose differently.

I stopped waiting for a better past and started creating a better future.

I released the version of life I thought I wanted so I could step into the one God was offering.

When you refuse to settle, you stop defining yourself by what broke you and start rebuilding from what is true.

The Reframe

In *Switch*, the Heath brothers teach that when people appear resistant to change, they are often simply unclear about what to do next. That truth mirrors the spiritual and emotional journey of every obstacle.

Obstacles will always appear, but they do not have the final word. When faced with honesty and faith, they become the very tools God uses to rebuild your strength.

Facing what's real doesn't close your story—it opens it.

It invites you to trade denial for direction, fear for faith, and confusion for clarity.

You do not have to have it all figured out. You only have to tell yourself the truth.

Because truth, even when it hurts, is the first step toward peace.

Reflection Prompts

- What obstacle in your life feels immovable right now?
- How could shifting your perspective bring peace, even if the circumstances do not change?
- How could facing your obstacle with honesty move you closer to freedom?

THIRTY-FOUR
RECLAIM YOUR POWER

Rise from What Tried to Break You

There are seasons when we lose sight of who we are.

After years of losses that stripped my identity and strength, I finally remembered who had the final word. I had been called many names: teen mom, divorced, bankrupt, sick. Somewhere along the way, I began to believe them. I forgot my true name. I forgot that I still had the authority to decide who I would become.

That was when I learned that **power lives in vulnerability.** The truth you hide keeps you bound. The truth you own sets you free.

Everything began to change when I finally understood this: if I do not reclaim my story, someone else will. And when others tell your story, they write it through their own lens, one that rarely captures the truth of who you are or the strength of what you have survived.

Reclaiming your power does not mean returning to who you were before everything fell apart. It means stepping forward with a deeper awareness of your worth, refusing to let your scars speak louder than your strength. Rising begins the moment you decide your story will no longer be written by what tried to break you.

Rediscovering Strength

For years, I lived to prove my worth, to be the reliable one, the achiever, the woman who could carry everything without breaking. But peace does not come from perfection. It comes from alignment.

When I began aligning my life with God's truth instead of others' expectations, I started to see myself clearly again. Reclaiming your power begins there: remembering whose you are before remembering who you are.

Everyone around you will try to define you. Family, colleagues, critics, even social media—they hand you labels, and if you are not careful, you begin to wear them. I wore them all. I let shame quiet my voice. I let betrayal convince me I was unworthy of trust. I let illness tell me I was weak.

But the power of your story is not in what happened to you. It is in what you choose to do with it.

When Faith Becomes the Anchor

Author Elizabeth George wrote in *Loving God with All Your Mind,*

"When you cannot see God's hand, trust His heart."

Those words became a lifeline for me.

There were days when I could not trace God in the chaos, when nothing around me made sense. But faith, I learned, is not the absence of fear. Faith keeps you walking when the outcome remains unseen.

That trust became my compass. I stopped looking back at what was lost and began moving toward what could still be redeemed.

Instead of replaying the pain, I began to rewrite the purpose. In time, I saw that even in my most broken moments, God's hand had never left me. I could not see it then, but He was writing a story I would one day have the courage to tell.

The Freedom of Surrender

True strength doesn't hide behind control — it **emerges through surrender.**

When you release the need to manage every outcome, you create space for God to move. That defines faith under pressure: trusting His heart stays good even when His hand feels hidden.

Reclaiming power never means forcing results. It means standing firm in uncertainty and choosing to believef that purpose can still rise from the pieces.

Each time I shared my story with raw honesty, another layer of shame fell away.

Then I realized something profound: people *gain strength through your transparency, not your performance.*

Your Turn to Rise

Owning your story **doesn't weaken you—it sets you free.**

Once you claim it fully, no one holds power to twist it against you.

I have seen this truth reflected in others:

• The woman who turned her grief into a ministry of hope.

• The leader who admitted failure and gained the respect she had been chasing for years.

• The mother who turned her hardest season into a testimony of grace.

Every time someone demonstrates vulnerability, light enters the room.

Reclaiming your power is not about control. It is about courage. It is about looking at your life—the heartbreak, the healing, and the hard lessons —and saying, *'This, too, will be used for good.'*

Reflection Prompts

- What label or lie have you believed that keeps you from standing in your true strength?
- How could surrendering control open space for God's power to work through your story?
- What truth, once spoken, would set you free?

THIRTY-FIVE

IGNITE RESILIENCE

Triumph Over Setbacks

Some seasons hit so hard they steal your breath. Betrayal upon betrayal. Dreams dissolving. A body that refuses to heal.

The night of my car accident in 2015, headlights filled my rearview mirror and time split in two. I believed the worst had ended once I climbed from the wreck, yet the months that followed revealed a different story. A traumatic brain injury, relentless migraines, and the silence of a darkened room pressed against my spirit until hope began to fade.

That season tempted me to stay buried—to let the setback define my story. But triumph grows through pain, not around it. You may fall into a pit, but you never belonged there.

The Setup Hidden in the Setback

Setbacks whisper lies: *You've failed. You've finished. You'll never recover.* When everything crumbles, believing the lie feels easier than trusting what you cannot see.

But setbacks become setups. They plant roots beneath the surface, nurturing unseen strength. Like a seed hidden in darkness, you may feel forgotten, yet growth quietly unfolds.

As I rested in that quiet room, unable to mother or work the way I longed to, something sacred began to stir. Stillness slowed my striving. Dependence deepened my faith. Growth took root even when nothing appeared to move.

Holding On When You Want to Let Go

Carol Kent wrote in *When I Lay My Isaac Down*, *"Sometimes faith isn't about having the strength to let go; it's about trusting God enough to keep holding on."*

Those words carried me through recovery and rebuilding. Faith rarely arrives as bold courage—it often appears as steady endurance, the quiet choice to keep showing up when everything inside you screams for escape.

When friendships faded, I learned release without resentment.

When silence stretched long, I learned to listen for God's whisper.

When my body faltered, I learned patience and dependence.

Each breaking birthed something new. Each ending introduced a beginning.

Turning Pain Into Purpose

Pain strips away illusion until only what's eternal remains. Every setback holds an invitation to grow beyond comfort. Safety feels familiar, but it rarely transforms you.

My sons watched me rise from my lowest point. They saw a mother fight for healing, for faith, for life itself. And because of that, they learned something I could never have taught with words: setbacks don't demand surrender.

Triumph rarely arrives through ease. It begins with the decision to rise again.

The Purpose Beneath the Pain

Pain often disguises the doorway to destiny. What feels like an ending often introduces who you're becoming—and reveals the God who redeems every broken thing.

Setbacks remain inevitable. Quitting stays optional.

When life knocks you flat, ask yourself:

Will this setback bury me, or will it plant me?

Triumph doesn't always roar. Sometimes it's the quiet act of getting out of bed when grief says, *stay down.*

Sometimes it's showing up for your children when your heart feels hollow.

Sometimes it's choosing forgiveness when bitterness promises comfort.

Each small act of perseverance becomes proof that purpose already grows within you.

Your story continues.

Your pain holds purpose.

God weaves every fragment into redemption.

And one day, your survival story will become someone else's saving grace.

Reflection Prompts

- What setback have you mistaken for an ending?
- How could you reframe it as preparation for something greater?

- What small triumph can you celebrate today, even in the middle of struggle?

THIRTY-SIX

TRANSFORM PURPOSE INTO IMPACT

Turn Compassion Into Calling

For years, I believed my story was too much — too dramatic, too complex, too complicated for people to carry. Or maybe it wasn't enough. I was never sure if the lows were low *enough* or if the highs were high *enough*. I thought I carried too much mess to help anyone. Now I see the mess itself as the very proof that redemption runs deeper than failure. I didn't realize transformation often begins in the stories we're most afraid to tell.

None of it looked like the stuff of inspiration. I assumed the stories that moved people belonged to those with tidy endings and polished platforms, people who had it all figured out.

But I guessed wrong.

The Night I Realized My Story Could Heal Someone Else

One evening in a small church group, everything I believed about my story began to change. I offered just a sliver—nervous, unsure, my voice barely steady. I expected awkward silence or maybe a polite nod. Instead, a woman I hardly knew walked up to me after the meeting, tears streaming down her cheeks. She leaned in and whispered, "Thank you. I thought I walked through this alone."

In that moment, I realized purpose could become impact: inspiration doesn't require a perfect ending. It comes from honesty. When we tell the truth—messy, unpolished, unfinished—we give others permission to believe that healing is possible for them too.

Truth Over Image: What People Really Need

We all want our stories to matter. But fear tells us to stay silent. It convinces us that vulnerability might cost us more than it gives. So we edit, polish, and hide the parts that still ache.

But silence doesn't protect us. It only isolates us.

The world doesn't need another highlight reel. It needs truth. Raw, honest truth that cuts through the noise and says, "You're not the only one." When I shared about betrayal, women stepped forward with their own buried pain. When I spoke of illness, others found the courage to seek help. When I admitted the shame of financial collapse, people in leadership finally exhaled and said, "Me too."

Each time I shared, someone else dared to hope. That's what real inspiration looks like—hope multiplied.

Empathy in Motion

Bestselling author of The Empathic Leader, Melissa Robinson-Winemiller, puts it this way:

"Empathy isn't just about feeling—it's about understanding. It's the bridge we build when we step into someone else's perspective. That bridge can be strong enough to move mountains, yet soft enough to hold another's heart."

You don't need a platform to have an impact. Sometimes, all it takes is a quiet conversation, a short message, or a few trembling words shared online. That small act might be someone else's lifeline.

You Don't Have to Wait Until It's Finished

Over time, I've seen what happens when we choose honesty over image. A college student told me my story helped her choose to keep her baby. A business owner said my vulnerability helped him keep going after financial ruin. A woman fighting chronic pain wrote that my words gave her the strength to face another day.

I didn't script those outcomes. I simply told the truth, and the truth did the work.

As Bob Goff writes in his book *Love Does*, "Love is never stationary. In the end, love doesn't just keep thinking about it or planning for it. Simply put: love does."

Every time we speak with empathy instead of fear and offer understanding instead of judgment, love moves.

You don't have to wait for a clean ending. You don't need to feel polished. Your story, exactly as it stands today, might be the light someone else needs to find their way forward. That's how purpose transforms into impact—when your healed places become hope for someone still in the fire.

Reflection Prompts

- Who in your life might be waiting for permission to hope again—and could your story give them that permission?
- What part of your journey have you been hiding that might be the key to helping someone else heal?
- How could you share your story in a way that feels honest, even if it's not perfect?

Discover Freedom in Daily Faithfulness

The morning after my final surgery in 2017, I woke up different.

For the first time in two years, I no longer felt trapped beneath migraines. The relentless pain had lifted. Freedom filled my lungs like air, like light, like possibility.

Yet healing did not mark a finish line.

Freedom did not arrive as a one-time victory.

If I wanted to live differently, I needed to choose differently—every single day.

Your rewrite never happens through a single decision. It unfolds through daily practice—a commitment renewed each time you wake up and decide to live in alignment with the story you are still becoming.

The Myth of the Moment

Many believe transformation begins with a breakthrough—the new job, the wedding day, the miracle. But real change rarely comes in a flash; it grows through maintenance.

Life tests progress. It calls you back toward old fears and familiar patterns. Without intention, you quietly drift into who you used to be.

Elevation requires vigilance. Truth told, courage chose, faith practiced—daily.

After surgery, I needed to decide not to live as though I remained sick. I rebuilt routines, reimagined purpose, and refused the comfort of smallness. The battle had not ended; it had simply changed form.

Transformation never removes struggle. It reshapes how you walk through it.

The Power of Daily Practice

John C. Maxwell wrote in *The 15 Invaluable Laws of Growth*, *"You'll never change your life until you change something you do daily."*

Those words became my anchor. At first, I believed transformation meant striving—pushing harder, chasing more, forcing outcomes. In time, I discovered that lasting change grows from peace within consistent rhythms.

Each morning became an act of surrender:

"God, I trust You with this day. With this story. With me."

That daily trust built strength one sunrise at a time.

If you long for freedom, choose freedom today.

If you crave strength, take the step strong people take today.

If you desire joy, practice gratitude today.

The life you want does not wait somewhere far away; it grows from the quiet choices you make right now.

Transformation in the Ordinary

Transformation often begins in moments that feel forgettable—

the morning you pray instead of panic,

the afternoon you forgive instead of resent,

the night you rest instead of reaching for distraction.

Those small decisions redirect your entire story. Ordinary choices, repeated faithfully, create extraordinary change.

I have witnessed this truth in countless lives:

The woman who spoke life over herself each morning until confidence felt natural.

The man who chose sobriety one day at a time until days became years.

The mother who showed up through grief until joy rose again like dawn.

None of them transformed overnight. They transformed daily.

The Rhythm of Renewal

Transformation rarely happens in the spotlight. It unfolds in hidden places—when no one sees you, and you still decide to keep going. Those unseen moments define who you become.

Your rewrite does not belong to a single chapter. It belongs to a rhythm.

A rhythm of grace.

Of choosing again.

Of trusting that slow progress still counts.

You will stumble. You may slip into old habits. Yet every sunrise invites you to begin again.

So today, choose elevation. Choose alignment. Choose to live as though your future already exists.

Because the rewrite never centers on your past. It unfolds through your present.

And when you live each day with intention, your future builds itself in faith.

Transformation never waits for perfect timing; you embody it now.

And when you do, your life becomes living proof that redemption remains possible.

Reflection Prompts

- What old story feels easiest to return to when life grows heavy?
- What daily habit could align you with the future you want to create?
- How might your life shift if you treated each sunrise as a second chance?

Want the exact reflection questions and frameworks that helped me turn trauma into transformation?

Scan this QR code to download the full R.E.W.R.I.T.E. Framework™ + EPIC System — the same tools I used to turn rock bottom into rocket fuel... and guide others through theirs.

Inside, you'll get:

☑ **Guided Reflection Questions** for every chapter in Parts I & II

☑ A one-page **R.E.W.R.I.T.E.™ Cheat Sheet** to reclaim your power

☑ The full **EPIC Framework** to turn healing into impact

These aren't just "nice to have" tools —

They're a **map back to yourself... and forward into purpose.**

Scan me!

Scan to Start Your Rewrite

(*Instant download. No spam. Just soul-level strategies that work.*)

➡ Or visit: **epicimpact.com**

PART 3

PART III THE EPIC FRAMEWORK™

WHEN YOUR STORY STOPS BEING ONLY
ABOUT YOU AND STARTS BECOMING THE
LANGUAGE OF HOPE FOR SOMEONE ELSE.

THIRTY-EIGHT

FROM REWRITE TO RIPPLE

How Sharing Your Story Deepens Healing

There comes a moment in every rewrite when your story stops being just yours. The pain that once left you speechless becomes the exact language someone else needs to hear.

That's when healing echoes—first inside you, then through you.

For me, it started in a quiet conference room in Greenville, South Carolina. I sat across from six men who had lived more life than most could imagine. Fathers scarred by trauma, addiction, incarceration, and loss. Men who had tasted rock bottom and fought their way back.

I didn't feel qualified to lead them.

But now I see it clearly: my story had been preparing me all along.

Parallel Pains, Shared Purpose

On the last day of kindergarten, a boy named Karriem Edwards lost his father to a heroin overdose in South Florida.

Years later, in upstate South Carolina, my two boys watched their own dad spiral into meth addiction and land in prison.

Different places. Different times. Same ache. Same unanswered questions.

Watching my sons carry wounds too deep for words shattered me. I prayed. I worked. I hoped healing would find them.

That pain nearly broke us.

But what began to save us was the act of rewriting our story.

Years later, that rewrite came full circle when I was invited to partner with the South Carolina Center for Fathers and Families. The man leading it? Karriem Edwards—the same boy who had once lost his father and now helped others become the fathers they never had.

Karriem turned his deepest wound into his life's mission: restoring fatherhood across the state. Together, we ran a storytelling workshop for six men in reentry. Karriem called them The Father Fellows.

I showed up thinking I was the teacher. But it didn't take long to realize I was there to learn, too.

When Storytelling Heals

Each man carried a heavy story—prison time, broken families, shame cycles. At first, they spoke with caution, their shoulders tense. But something shifted as they opened up. Their stories stopped sounding like confessions and started sounding like bridges.

Not speeches. Not performances. Just truth. Spoken aloud in a room that could finally hold it.

One of them, William, spoke quietly, almost to himself:

"It was therapeutic... I actually didn't even have to go to therapy. It opened up everything I needed to say. And I was around the right people to say it to."

That moment stayed with me because I knew exactly what he meant.

When I first shared the truth of my own story—becoming a teen mom, surviving betrayal, rebuilding after trauma—I felt the same release.

It wasn't about spotlight. It was about peace.

That's what story does. It gives you back the parts pain tried to erase.

The Power of Structure

To guide their stories, I introduced two simple frameworks:

• The R.E.W.R.I.T.E. Process – for finding meaning in pain.

• The EPIC Framework™ – for sharing that meaning in a powerful, honest way.

What happened next wasn't about strategy. It was sacred.

In just a few hours, six men who had once seen themselves as failures started seeing themselves as fathers, leaders, and advocates. They stopped telling stories about what happened *to* them. They started owning what was happening *through* them.

That's the power of The R.E.W.R.I.T.E. Framework. It rebuilds identity. That's what EPIC does. It gives your voice volume.

Together, they do more than heal individuals. They start healing communities.

The Ripple Takes Root

Three weeks later, I returned for the follow-up. Transformation had grown into something bigger. Multiplication.

Nicholas and James had already spoken on the local news. William prepped for another media interview. Pierre was set to speak at a community event.

Each of them called that workshop a turning point.

Dr. Lawrence E. Ford, Sr., the Center's Director of Communications, said:

> *"Nicholas didn't know what the interview was going to be about. But I could tell he had practiced. He knew what he wanted to say. He had written it out and was spot on."*

They didn't memorize scripts. They shared stories. They didn't recite talking points. They offered lived experience.

As Karriem put it:

> *"You guys began to bond... it was all totally subliminal, and everybody did it by natural response."*

Healing sparked brotherhood. Brotherhood sparked movement. All from one shared story.

Healing Grows When It's Shared

That's the ripple of healing—it begins as a whisper and builds into a wave.

When you share your story, you give others permission to find theirs.

William said it best:

"I just go home and do things differently now. I'm excited."

That's the power of choosing to stop being a silent survivor and start showing up as a storyteller. As a change-maker.

Every time you speak truth in love, you strengthen the healed parts of you—and light the way for someone else.

From Survivor to Storyteller

You don't need a stage to speak. You don't need a title to lead.

Your voice carries weight because it proves you made it through.

The healing you've found wasn't meant to stay bottled up. It's meant to flow—through your words, your empathy, and your courage.

That's what The R.E.W.R.I.T.E. is really about. You weren't buried. You were planted.

The Turning Point Between Healing and Sharing

Here's what I learned in that room:

You don't need to be polished to be powerful. You just need to be honest about your transformation.

Your story was never meant to stop with you. It's meant to move through you.

That's how you multiply your rewrite:

• Use your healing to help someone else heal.

• Use your voice to lift someone else's burden.

• Use your story as light in someone else's dark.

The moment you speak, your pain becomes the language someone else has been waiting for.

Because in the end, your greatest impact won't come from having the perfect story. It will come from sharing it.

That's what The Rewrite makes possible: It takes what once crushed you and turns it into a message that sets others free.

And that's where the next chapter begins.

The same structure that helped me rebuild my life is what helped me share it. It turned my private restoration into public impact.

That framework is called EPIC. And it's how your healing becomes hope for others.

Reflective Questions

- Who could be changed by the part of your story you're still hiding?
- Could your greatest wound be someone else's breakthrough?
- What would it look like if your healing became someone else's hope?

THIRTY-NINE

EPIC—THE FRAMEWORK THAT TURNS HEALING INTO IMPACT

How to Share Your Story with Purpose, Power, and Heart

Some stories end at survival. Others ripple into healing.

Luck changes nothing. Structure changes everything.

When I first started sharing pieces of my story—teen motherhood, betrayal, loss, recovery—I noticed something. Every time I led with honesty instead of perfection, people leaned in. When I told the truth about pain and paired it with hope, hearts opened.

Still, I didn't fully understand why some stories healed while others only inspired. That changed when I tested what worked.

Over the past few years, I've used this storytelling approach—now called The EPIC Framework™—across hundreds of talks, posts, and campaigns. Since then, my email open rates have doubled. My book hit #1 on Amazon. My storytelling won writing awards. More importantly, I've seen people use it to speak their truth with peace instead of panic.

EPIC never stops at communication. It creates connection that respects both emotion and transformation.

Why EPIC Matters for Trauma Survivors

Most storytelling advice teaches performance. EPIC teaches processing.

It's not about going viral or sounding polished. It's about learning to hold your story safely so it doesn't hold you hostage.

EPIC gives language to lived experience and structure to deep emotion. It helps you speak with clarity and confidence, even when you feel hesitant.

Whether you're on a stage or with a trusted friend, EPIC mirrors how healing unfolds: Connection first. Truth next. Hope in the middle. Clarity at the end.

The Power of Framework Over Formulas

Most communication systems focus on transactions. They teach you how to sell or persuade.

EPIC focuses on transformation. It teaches how to connect and heal.

It doesn't manipulate. It mirrors empathy. It doesn't pressure. It invites. It doesn't sell. It serves.

If you've lived through trauma, your nervous system craves safety to speak. EPIC provides that safety through sequence. You share what happened without spiraling back into it. You begin with empathy, ground your story in truth, and end with empowerment.

That's what sets EPIC apart. It's not performance. It's peace.

The EPIC Framework™

A Four-Part Flow for Telling the Truth Safely and Powerfully

Each stage mirrors a step in authentic connection and healing:

E — Engage with Empathy

Purpose: Start with empathy. Reflect emotion before explanation.

Question It Answers: *"Why should I listen?"*

Tip: Begin with a real moment. Use sensory detail—a smell, a sound, a setting. Ground your story in specificity.

Before: *"I used to struggle with anxiety."*

After: *"I remember lying awake at night, replaying every failure in my head, wondering if peace was something other people got to have."*

In your healing story: Don't open with victory. Start with vulnerability. Say, "I've been there too."

P — Persuade Through Vulnerability

Purpose: Build trust through truth. Pair what you felt with what you learned.

Question It Answers: *"Why should I believe healing is possible?"*

Tip: Show emotion without exaggeration. Highlight the turning point—what shifted inside you. Let details earn trust; let emotion make it stick.

Before: *"Eventually, I forgave."*

After: *"Forgiveness didn't come in one prayer. It came in a thousand small choices to release what was poisoning me."*

In your healing story: Show the process, not the perfection. People relate to your becoming—not your arrival.

I — Inspire with Vision

Purpose: Connect personal pain to a larger purpose.

Question It Answers: *"How does this connect to something bigger than me?"*

Tip: Show the ripple. Paint how healing opened space for purpose, empathy, or advocacy.

Before: *"Now I help others heal."*

After: *"What once nearly broke me now helps others believe they can rebuild too."*

In your healing story: Let your scars lead to someone else's hope. That's how pain becomes purpose.

C — Close with Clarity and Compassion

Purpose: End with hope. Offer one next step—reflection, connection, or action.

Question It Answers: *"What should I do next?"*

Tip: Bring it full circle. Return to where you began and show how it changed.

Before: *"So that's my story."*

After: *"If you're in that place too, please know you won't stay there forever."*

In your healing story: Don't end on the wound. End on the wisdom. Let your close become a bridge to hope.

How EPIC Complements R.E.W.R.I.T.E.

If the **R.E.W.R.I.T.E. Framework™** helped you heal your *inner* story, the **EPIC Framework™** helps you share that healing with the *outer* world.

REWRITE Focus	EPIC Expression
Reframe Pain	Engage with empathy
Embrace Reality	Persuade through vulnerability
Work Through Obstacles	Inspire with vision
Reclaim Power	Close with clarity and compassion

REWRITE transforms your heart.

EPIC helps you use that healed heart to help others.

The Proof: Why I Know EPIC Works

Since I began using EPIC, I've watched it shift everything—from inboxes to identities.

My open rates passed 92 percent because **real stories** beat rehearsed messages.

Nonprofits I've coached tripled engagement by focusing on **people, not stats**.

Survivors who once trembled with shame now share in groups, on stages, and one-on-one—with **clarity** they never expected to find.

This goes beyond communication. This builds connection that heals.

Your Message Is Your Mission in Motion

Your story does more than share what happened. It shows how you healed—and how you now hold space for others to heal too.

Every conversation, post, or coffee chat creates a bridge. Every time you speak truth without shame, you invite someone else to do the same.

EPIC helps you do that safely, simply, and sincerely.

. . .

Your Turn: Begin Your EPIC Rewrite

Start small:

- Choose one story you've been afraid to share.
- Write it using the EPIC flow: Engage → Persuade → Inspire → Close.
- Share it safely—with a counselor, a small group, or a trusted friend.

Watch what happens when your truth finds its voice. Every time you share from healing, you don't lose a piece of yourself—you gain peace.

Reflection Prompts

- What part of your story still feels too heavy to say out loud? What might lighten when you name it?
- Who in your life needs to hear the truth you've carried in silence?
- What would it look like to end your next story not in pain, but in purpose?

Your rewrite gave you healing.

EPIC helps you give that healing away.

The story that once broke you might be the one that sets someone else free.

FORTY

THE FUTURE OF STORYTELLING WITH AI

Where Healing Meets Innovation—and How the EPIC Impact™ App Brings It to Life

The room held sixty nonprofit leaders, and I could feel the skepticism in the air.

Another workshop. Another consultant. Another promise that *this time will be different.*

Lakesha McCutchen from the Spartanburg County Foundation had organized this training because she was "desperately searching for the right consultant" who could equip their local nonprofits with real storytelling skills. Their challenge was one I've heard countless times before: no staff, no time, no budget—and too many stories left untold.

I asked for a volunteer.

Larry raised his hand. He shared how his 14-year-old son, Christopher, had taken his own life in 2019. Christopher was funny, handsome, and when he smiled, it lit up the room. In the wake of their unimaginable loss, Larry and his wife Cathy made a promise: to do everything in their power to ensure no family would go through what they had experienced. That promise became **Christopher's Hope Foundation**, the first to bring *Hope Squad* peer intervention programs to South Carolina schools.

I had prepared twenty simple storytelling questions. Larry wrote his answers honestly—no polish, no marketing fluff. Then, during the demo, I ran his responses through the **EPIC Framework™**.

Minutes later, I read his rewritten story aloud.

The room went silent.

Here was Larry's grief—transformed into purpose. His story became a beacon of hope, showing how one family's pain could lead to prevention programs now in 26 schools across three counties.

"There was one specific moment during the workshop when I knew this training would make a real difference," Lakesha reflected. "When Hailey showed them how she rewrote Larry's story and brought it to life, you could see lightbulb moments happening all around the room. It really showed them that effective storytelling is as simple as 1, 2, 3."

That's what this chapter is about.

Not a world where AI replaces human connection—but one where **technology makes healing stories accessible to anyone with a mission worth sharing.**

The Revolution That's Already Here

Lakesha explained it best:

"Many of our nonprofit partners were requesting more training in marketing and communications, yet most didn't have dedicated staff for these critical functions."

The **EPIC Framework™** gave them structure. But when paired with AI, it did something even greater—it turned storytelling from *impossible* to *doable*.

That insight became the foundation for what's next:

The **EPIC Impact™ App** — where the power of storytelling meets the potential of artificial intelligence.

Beyond Generic AI: The EPIC Impact™ Difference

While the internet is crowded with generic AI writing tools, **EPIC Impact™** was built for something deeper.

It's not designed to write *for* you—it's designed to help you write *as* you.

EPIC Impact™ combines the proven psychology of the **EPIC Framework™**—Engage, Persuade, Inspire, Close—with intelligent AI guidance to help you find your voice, share your story, and scale your mission without losing authenticity.

Framework-Driven Intelligence

Most AI tools understand language.

EPIC Impact™ understands *story structure*.

It knows the difference between an *engagement hook* and an *inspiration moment*. It senses when your message needs more empathy, clarity, or courage—and gently helps you refine it.

Voice Clarification, Not Replacement

The Spartanburg leaders didn't need AI to think for them. They needed it to help them express what was already in their hearts.

EPIC Impact™ learns your voice, your mission, and your audience— then helps you communicate with more impact and less effort.

As Lakesha later said,

"Our nonprofits now use practical tools to attract more participants, volunteers, supporters, and funders through powerful storytelling. They no longer hope their stories will connect—they understand how to make deep connection happen."

That's the future of communication: *authentic stories, amplified by smart technology.*

Why EPIC Impact™ Works

Connect on a Deeper Level

Use emotionally intelligent storytelling to engage hearts and minds— no matter your audience.

Inspire Action, Fast

Drive more donations, decisions, and connection—without spending days crafting the perfect message.

Stay Consistent and On-Brand

Unify your voice across every email, post, and presentation.

Gain Clarity and Confidence—Every Time

Skip the blank page. Follow a proven framework that gives you both structure and freedom.

How It Works

1 Tell Us Your Goal — Choose your message type: donor appeal, client story, leadership talk, personal testimony, email, or social media.

2 Use the EPIC Prompt — Follow the guided flow: Engage, Persuade, Inspire, Close.

3 Review AI Suggestions — Get emotionally aware drafts you can refine to sound exactly like you.

4 Launch with Confidence — Post, pitch, or present your story —knowing it connects and compels.

Your Next Step: Experience EPIC in Action

If the **REWRITE Framework™** helped you heal your inner story,

the **EPIC Framework™**—and now, the **EPIC Impact™ App** —will help you *share it.*

You've learned how to turn pain into purpose.

Now it's time to turn that purpose into impact.

See the framework in action or join early access at

☞ **EpicImpact.ai**

You'll find live demos, free tools, and an exclusive community of mission-driven storytellers like you.

Whether you're rebuilding after loss, leading a cause, or growing a business with heart—EPIC Impact™ helps you craft messages that move people *and* move the mission forward.

The Next Chapter of Storytelling

Where Humanity Meets Technology — and Stories Find New Life

Lakesha McCutchen and her sixty nonprofit leaders proved something powerful:

When people receive the right framework and tools, they do not simply learn to tell better stories—they discover they have carried powerful stories all along.

The **EPIC Framework™** provides the structure.

AI provides the acceleration.

Your voice provides the heart.

Together, they create something extraordinary:

a world where every survivor, leader, and changemaker can share their truth—and make it EPIC.

This is the future of communication:

human stories powered by ethical intelligence.

☞ Visit **EpicImpact.ai** to see how story and AI are shaping what comes next.

Because your next story holds power. It could be the one that unlocks connection, trust, and transformation.

Are you ready to create your EPIC Impact™?

Your story starts now.

Want the exact reflection questions and frameworks that helped me turn trauma into transformation?

Scan this QR code to download the full R.E.W.R.I.T.E. Framework™ + EPIC System — the same tools I used to turn rock bottom into rocket fuel... and guide others through theirs.

. . .

Inside, you'll get:

☑ **Guided Reflection Questions** for every chapter in Parts I & II

☑ A one-page **R.E.W.R.I.T.E.™ Cheat Sheet** to reclaim your power

☑ The full **EPIC Framework** to turn healing into impact

These aren't just "nice to have" tools —

They're a **map back to yourself... and forward into purpose.**

Scan me!

Scan to Start Your Rewrite

(Instant download. No spam. Just soul-level strategies that work.)

➡ Or visit: **epicimpact.com**

APPENDIX: R.E.W.R.I.T.E. FRAMEWORK

Letter / Chapter	Core Focus	Emotional Objective	Spiritual / Mindset Shift	Practical Takeaway	Key Elements to Include
R – Reframe Your Pain *Find Meaning in the Breaking*	Perspective Shift	Help readers see pain as preparation, not punishment.	"If I can't change my circumstances, I can change my mindset — and that changes everything."	Write one lesson your pain has taught you and how it shaped your perspective.	Opening story of loss or collapse (pregnancy, betrayal, illness) · Introduce victim vs. victor mentality · Shift focus from "why me?" to "what now?" · Emphasize pain as a teacher · Tone: empathetic, reflective, empowering
E – Embrace Reality *Stand With Courage Where You Are*	Radical Acceptance	Guide readers from denial to peace through honesty and presence.	"Peace begins where pretending ends."	Write one sentence that names your current reality without judgment or justification.	Scene of surrender or truth-telling moment · Show that facing truth brings freedom, not failure · Include grounding practices (breathing, prayer, stillness) · Quote ideas: "You can't heal what you hide." / "Acceptance isn't giving up — it's growing up."
W – Work Through Obstacles *Choose Renewal Over Captivity*	Resilience in Action	Encourage steady, faithful progress when healing feels slow or uncertain.	"You don't have to move fast. You just have to move faithfully."	Choose one small daily action that represents progress, even if imperfect.	Symbolic imagery of motion (running, building, planting) · Show the "messy middle" without shame · Blend vulnerability (memoir) with clarity (practical action) · Include affirmation "Progress is proof that pain didn't win."
R – Reclaim Your Power *Rise from What Tried to Break You*	Identity & Agency	Empower readers to stop living defined by what broke them.	"You were a victim of what happened — but you don't have to live as one."	Write a declaration of power: "Today, I reclaim my voice by…"	Turning point story of choice or confrontation ("No more") · Define victim vs. victorious mindset · Reflection: "What can I control today?" · Quote: "You can't change your past, but you can change your posture." · Tone: bold, freeing, confident.
I – Ignite Resilience *Triumph Over Setbacks*	Faith-Fueled Endurance	Show that triumph grows through pain, not around it.	"What feels like breaking may be God building something deeper within you."	Identify one area where you can persevere today, even when it feels pointless.	Story of physical/emotional trial (car accident, illness, setback) · Reinforce faith and perseverance · Include quote: "Sometimes faith isn't strength to let go — it's trusting God enough to keep holding on." · Emphasize small daily triumphs as evidence of transformation · Tone: redemptive, steady, strong.
T – Transform Purpose into Impact *Turn Compassion Into Calling*	Purpose & Service	Help readers see that their healed places can heal others.	"Your story can set someone else free."	Identify one way your story could encourage or serve another person this week.	Story of sharing your truth and seeing it help others · Emphasize honesty over image · Tie empathy to mission ("Love moves.") · Quote: "Love is never stationary; it does." (Bob Goff). · Tone: authentic, relational, service-minded.
E – Embody Transformation *Discover Freedom in Daily Faithfulness*	Integration & Renewal	Teach readers to live healed — not as an event, but as a daily rhythm.	"Wholeness isn't a destination; it's a daily decision."	Create one daily rhythm that reflects your transformation (gratitude, journaling, prayer, kindness).	Imagery of ordinary faith (morning quiet, sunrise, laughter) · Reinforce consistency over perfection · Emphasize that transformation unfolds through daily alignment · Quote: "Transformation doesn't happen after the pain — it happens through it." · Tone: peaceful, mature, hopeful.

THANK YOU FOR READING REWRITE THE STORY THAT TRIED TO BREAK YOU AND TURN IT INTO STRATEGIES THAT STICK®

Your review changes lives. Ready to take your impact to the next level?

You did it.

You made it through every story, every framework, every reflection that asked you to look deeper, to heal harder, and to believe again.

As someone who knows what it means to live through breaking and begin again, I can't tell you how much it means that you trusted me—and these words—with your own journey.

But here's the truth: your rewrite doesn't end here.

It's just beginning.

Before you go out and live your next chapter, I have one small favor to ask.

Your Words Could Change Another Survivor's Life

If this book helped you in any way—if it gave you language for your pain, permission to heal, or hope that you can still write a new ending —would you consider leaving a review?

Reviews do more than sit on a page. They build trust and drive action. They're how other people who are searching for healing stories find the right book at the right time.

Your words might be the reason someone else finally believes that redemption is possible.

As an author, your feedback helps me continue this mission—to give more people the tools to transform pain into purpose.

Your encouragement truly keeps me going on the hard days.

Where to Leave Reviews:

• **Amazon** – Even if you didn't purchase there, you can still leave a review with an Amazon account.

• **Goodreads** – The world's largest community of readers.

• **Barnes & Noble** – Online reviews welcomed from all readers.

• **Social media** – Share your favorite quote or biggest takeaway with your community.

Even one line—like *"This book helped me see my pain differently"*— can help someone else find the courage to begin their rewrite.

Gift It Forward

Know someone walking through their own breaking? Someone who needs to believe their story is not over?

Pass this book along.

Sometimes the most powerful gift is not advice or solutions—it is belief. The kind that says, *"Healing still lives here."*

Ready to Take Your Rewrite to the Next Level?

If this book resonated with you and you're ready to amplify your story, my bestselling follow-up,

EPIC Impact™: Transform Your Message Into a Movement, shows you how to create magnetic stories that influence, inspire action, and lead with authenticity.

EPIC Impact™ became an **Amazon #1 Bestseller** in *Nonprofit Marketing, Leadership & Management,* and *Grants & Fundraising,* helping changemakers and survivors alike communicate their purpose with clarity, confidence, and compassion.

Visit **epicimpact.ai** to see how story + AI can help you craft messages that move people.

Or, if you'd like to work with me personally:

• **Workshops & Keynotes:** Story-driven sessions to help teams and individuals share their stories with purpose and impact.

• **EPIC Impact™ App:** Create authentic, powerful storytelling content in minutes.

• **EPIC Impact™ Community:** A supportive network of mission-driven leaders rewriting their worlds through story.

You're Not Just a Reader. You're Part of the Movement.

Remember the heartbeat of this book:

You are just one story away from breakthrough.

Now you carry the tools to live it, speak it, and share it.

The world needs your voice, your empathy, your courage to keep showing up as yourself.

When you see your story begin to ripple out and change lives (because it will), I'd love to hear from you.

Reach me anytime at **hailey@haileyevans.com**, or connect online:

• **Facebook**

• **LinkedIn**

• **Instagram**

• **YouTube**

• **Amazon Author Page**

Thank you for trusting me with your story.

Thank you for believing that healing—and rewriting—are still possible.

Now go live your next chapter.

You're just one story away,

Hailey Evans

P.S. - If EPIC or R.E.W.R.I.T.E. feel overwhelming, start with one real message this week. Choose something you already plan to write. Apply either framework. Then observe what shifts. Small, intentional moves lead to real momentum.

Want the exact reflection questions and frameworks that helped me turn trauma into transformation?

Scan this QR code to download the full R.E.W.R.I.T.E. Framework™ + EPIC System — the same tools I used to turn rock bottom into rocket fuel… and guide others through theirs.

Inside, you'll get:

☑ **Guided Reflection Questions** for every chapter in Parts I & II

☑ A one-page **R.E.W.R.I.T.E.™ Cheat Sheet** to reclaim your power

☑ The full **EPIC Framework** to turn healing into impact

These aren't just "nice to have" tools —

They're a **map back to yourself... and forward into purpose.**

Scan me!

Scan to Start Your Rewrite

(Instant download. No spam. Just soul-level strategies that work.)

➡ Or visit: **epicimpact.com**

REFERENCES

31 – Reframe Your Pain

Frankl, Viktor E. Man's Search for Meaning. Boston: Beacon Press,

1959.

32 – Embrace Reality

Moore, Beth. Chasing Vines: Finding Your Way to an Immensely

Fruitful Life. Carol Stream, IL: Tyndale House Publishers, 2020.

33 – Work Through Obstacles

Heath, Chip, and Dan Heath. Switch: How to Change
Things When

Change Is Hard. New York: Broadway Books, 2010.

34 – Reclaim Your Power

George, Elizabeth. Loving God with All Your Mind. Eugene, OR:

Harvest House Publishers, 1994.

35 – Ignite Resilience

Kent, Carol. When I Lay My Isaac Down: Unshakable Faith in

Unthinkable Circumstances. Colorado Springs, CO: NavPress, 2004.

36 – Transform Purpose into Impact

Robinson-WineMiller, Melissa. The Empathetic Leader: How to Lead

Electively by Caring Deeply. Nashville, TN: Thomas Nelson, 2023.

Go!, Bob. Love Does: Discover a Secretly Incredible Life in an Ordinary World. Nashville, TN: Thomas Nelson, 2012.

37 – Embody Transformation

Maxwell, John C. The 15 Invaluable Laws of Growth: Live Them

and Reach Your Potential. New York: Center Street, 201

38 — From Rewrite to Ripple

Edwards, Karriem — President, South Carolina Center for Fathers and Families; shared his personal story and leadership insights featured in the chapter.

Ford, Dr. Lawrence E., Sr., D.Min. — Director of Marketing and Communications, South Carolina Center for Fathers and Families; provided commentary on participant media readiness.

South Carolina Center for Fathers and Families — Nonprofit organization featured in the chapter for its Father Fellows program and ambassador development.

William — Father Fellow participant in the EPIC storytelling workshop; shared his testimony of healing and advocacy.

Nicholas — Father Fellow participant who shared his story in media interviews after the EPIC workshop.

James — Father Fellow participant featured for his advocacy efforts post-workshop.

Pierre — Father Fellow participant highlighted for his speaking engagements and reflections on AI-assisted storytelling.

40 — The Future of Storytelling with AI

Lawrence, Larry — Workshop participant who shared his personal story of loss and founded Christopher's Hope Foundation.

Lawrence, Cathy — Co-founder of Christopher's Hope Foundation, in memory of her son Christopher.

McCutchen, Lakesha — Community Engagement Officer, Spartanburg County Foundation; organized the workshop featured in the chapter and provided reflections.

Spartanburg County Foundation — Nonprofit organization that hosted the nonprofit storytelling + AI training featured in the chapter.

Christopher's Hope Foundation — Nonprofit founded by Larry and Cathy Lawrence in memory of their son, featured as a case study in the chapter.

Hope Squad — Peer intervention program sponsored in South Carolina schools by Christopher's Hope Foundation.

www.ingramcontent.com/pod-product-compliance
Lightning Source LLC
Chambersburg PA
CBHW071157210326
41597CB00016B/1579